Congress at the Grassroots

Congress
at the *Grassroots*

Representational
Change in the South,
1970–1998

Richard F. Fenno Jr.

The University of
North Carolina Press
Chapel Hill and London

© 2000 The University of North Carolina Press
All rights reserved
Manufactured in the United States of America
Designed by April Leidig-Higgins
Set in Electra by Keystone Typesetting, Inc.

The paper in this book meets the guidelines for
permanence and durability of the Committee on
Production Guidelines for Book Longevity of the
Council on Library Resources.

Library of Congress Cataloging-in-Publication Data
Fenno, Richard F., 1926–   Congress at the
grassroots : representational change in the South,
1970–1998 / Richard F. Fenno, Jr.
p. cm. Includes bibliographical references (p.   )
and index.
ISBN 0-8078-2542-5 (alk. paper)
ISBN 0-8078-4855-7 (pbk.: alk. paper)
1. United States. Congress. House. 2. Legislators—
United States—Case studies. 3. Representative
government and representation—United States—
Case studies. 4. Georgia—Politics and government—
1951–   . I. Title.
JK1319.F43 2000   328.73′092′2—dc21   99-055915

cloth   05 04 03 02 01   5 4 3 2 1
paper   07 06 05 04 03   7 6 5 4 3

To Lib

Contents

Maps and Tables

Preface

This book is about political change in America as reflected in changing patterns of representation. The research focus is on two members of the U.S. House of Representatives, each of whom represented the same district, but at different points in time, one from the 1950s to the 1970s, the other in the 1990s. The research question is threefold. First, what, if anything, has changed in the way in which the two House members have gone about the job of representing their constituents? Second, how might we explain this change? And third, how might the explanation of this change help us to explain representational change more generally?

The research approach is based on the idea that representation is a process; that it is, in part, a grassroots process; and that questions of representational change can therefore usefully be studied at the grassroots level. The research strategy is one of on-the-scene personal observation of the two representatives at work in a congressional district in west-central Georgia, just south of Atlanta.

While the study is directly about representational change in one district, the hope is that it might also contribute to the larger subject of political change in the South. District-level change—from a mostly rural, one-party Democratic district to a mostly suburban, Republican-dominated one—surely has relevance for the study of political change in the region. A further hope is that in its conceptualization and focus—if not in its scope—the study might contribute something to the larger study of political change nationwide. It might, for example, help us to understand the increasingly polarized partisanship we have been observing in the House of Representatives in Washington.

The years preceding the new millennium have not been friendly to America's politicians. As a group, they have been ranked near the bottom of the ladder of occupational respect. As individuals, they have not been held up as role models. More parents than ever are advising their children not to go into politics. Why, then, it might be asked, would anyone want to write about two individual politicians? Or, more to the point, why would anyone want to read about them? Newspaper editors and television producers do not find such individuals interesting or newsworthy—unless they are touched by scandal. And political scientists tend to fold individual politicians into large data sets—unless they hold leadership positions.

The simplest reason for studying politicians is that however much they are demeaned and denounced, and however uneventful and unimportant their everyday activity may seem to be, they are people without whom our democracy cannot work. And since we have a representative democracy, it seems only reasonable and prudent to take a look, occasionally, at a few of those who make democracy work—and to look at them where they work. It also makes sense to see them as flesh-and-blood, multidimensional individuals and not just as part of a widely condemned category of "politicians."

Representation is both a grand idea for our political system and a grassroots activity for our individual representatives. If readers can capture a sense of the latter, perhaps they will strengthen their grasp of the former. Overwhelmingly and deliberately, therefore, the focus of this study is on the grassroots activity. The reader will be overloaded with information about the day-to-day, district-level activities of two little-known House members. Why? Because the study makes a basic distinction between the representational patterns of the two House members, a distinction that is based mostly on evidence from seven personal visits and twenty-five days spent in the district, and I want to convince the reader of the validity of the distinction. Readers will therefore be exposed to the fullest range of the raw evidence— that they may see, feel, and weigh it for themselves.

The book will take the reader to the counties, the towns, the homes, the businesses, the churches, the schools, the rallies, the meetings, the restaurants, the coffee shops, the clubs, the organizations, the fields, the streets, and the parks—event by event, handshake by handshake, friend by friend, group by group, visit by visit, question by question, answer by answer, story by story. The research required considerable stamina and patience. Readers will need stamina and patience, too.

Given the goal of reader immersion, the chronological narrative form seemed appropriate. This form, of course, makes the author responsible for selecting, organizing, and presenting the material.

Admittedly, I have done that in ways that suggest and support certain generalizations about individual patterns of representation and about changes in these patterns. But I have tried to be faithful to the material and not to distort the presentation of it or press it to do more than is warranted by the evidence. In no sense is there any idea that one person's pattern is "better" than the other's, only that they are explainably "different." The methodological problems that are endemic to this kind of participant-observation research and my own efforts to cope with them have been discussed at length elsewhere.

My debt to those who have made this book possible begins with the two principals, Jack Flynt and Mac Collins. Both men were candid and accommodating, altogether a pleasure to be with, talk with, and learn from. They wanted to help, and they did—a lucky combination for me. Each has read and commented, encouragingly, on his portion of the manuscript. And each has been helpful in correcting some factual mistakes. But the data, interpretations, and judgments are wholly my responsibility.

Without the graciousness of Patty Flynt and Julie Collins, too, my district visits would have been less profitable than they were.

Among Jack Flynt's staff, I owe thanks for their assistance to Mary Lou (Lucas) Smalley, Rae Joiner, and the late Joe Akin. Among Mac Collins's staffers, my special debt is to Shirley Gillespie and Clark Reid, whose generous welcome and assistance were indispensable to my work in the district. Betty Munro was a versatile friend, both in the district and in Washington. My tasks in Georgia were lightened, in all sorts of ways, by Betty Bush, Fred Chitwood, Lisa Parrish, Wanda Tscudy, and Jean Studdard. In Washington I received friendly assistance from Sari Greenberg, Brian Jones, Kirk Foster, Ann Jasien, and Bo Bryant. I thank them all.

I am much indebted to three expert colleagues for their stimulation, guidance, and all-around sustenance—Merle Black, Chuck Bullock, and Harold Stanley. I could not have ventured into this project without being able to lean on their knowledge, counsel, and friendship. Merle Black not only read the manuscript but put his own neck on the line by recommending me to a publisher! My thanks to Gary Jacobson and Gerald Gamm for reading the manuscript and making helpful suggestions. I also thank Bill Bianco and Tom Mann for their comments.

With respect to my publisher, the University of North Carolina Press, and with respect to my editors there, I can only say I have been most fortunate. I thank Lewis Bateman for his strong support. I also thank Paula Wald for her reassuring in-house management and Mary Reid for her expert copyediting.

I dedicate the book, with affection, to my sister Elizabeth Blucke, who steered me to my first teaching job and who has supported me all the way to Georgia.

Congress at the Grassroots

CHAPTER ONE

Political Representation

Background

When Newt Gingrich emerged full-blown onto the American political stage in the 1990s, he carried with him into public view a little-
known political figure named John J. Flynt Jr.—not into the bright
lights of center stage, to be sure, but into the dim background, as a bit
player to be hustled onto the stage, briefly noted, and hustled off
again. Flynt was the incumbent Georgia congressman who twice
defeated the aspiring young Gingrich—first in 1974 and again in
1976—and whose retirement in 1978 propelled the Republican college professor into Congress.

Reporters who inquired into Gingrich's early career, therefore,
discovered Jack Flynt. They characterized him succinctly as a "longtime conservative Democratic congressman," "an ageing incumbent
Dixiecrat," "a standard bearer of the old courthouse crowds."[1] The
reporters contented themselves with these thumbnail characteriza-
tions and moved on. They knew nothing about Flynt; he was not
their story. I do know something about him, and I want to make him
the centerpiece of my story—a story about changing patterns of representation in the U.S. House of Representatives.

Three times in the 1970s (1970, 1972, and 1976), I went to Georgia
to follow Jack Flynt as he worked in his district. Eventually he became a leading character in my study, *Home Style*.[2] In the twenty
years since that study was published, however, much has changed in
American politics. As I thought about that change, it occurred to me
that my constituency-level explorations in the 1970s had given me

some unique baselines from which to begin to explore changes in the relationships between House members and their constituencies. It seemed to me, further, that such an exploration might profitably begin in a constituency where some easily recognizable macro-level political changes had occurred—and that one obvious place was the South. These reflections led me to think about revisiting my travels with southerner Jack Flynt, and to think about using that experience to construct a baseline from which to explore micro-level political change in the region.

When I dug out my notes, I found two baselines. The first allowed me to explore changing representational relationships over the course of Flynt's own twenty-year incumbency, during which his small-town, rural district changed into a suburban district. There the question was, How might a House member with well-established constituency connections react to the challenge of contextual changes over which the member has no control? The second baseline encouraged me to explore the change in representational relationships between Flynt's incumbency in the 1970s and the incumbency of a successor in the 1990s. And so, four times in the 1990s (twice in 1996 and twice in 1998), I returned to the old Flynt district—that is, to the remaining three-quarters to two-thirds of it—to travel with its current representative, Mac Collins. Here the question was, In what ways, and why, might the representational relationships of two different House members in the same district have changed from the 1970s to the 1990s?

This book, therefore, tells two stories about representation. Both stories involve a single district in the South, and each one covers nearly a quarter of a century. They are liable to all the sampling infirmities and scientific inadequacies of a case study. They are a first-cut, narrative account of one instance of representational change. Whether or not the narrative has anything to say about representational change in general, or about representational change in the South, or representational change in a suburbanizing type of district, I cannot say. But it might. At the least, it will put a human face on one of the most profound changes in recent American politics. And it will provide some individual-level support for larger generalizations about political change in the South. At the most, it might stimulate further micro-level examination of the larger subject of political representation.

Conceptualization

Representation is surely one of the most multifaceted ideas in political science. Not surprisingly, therefore, the study of political representation has been as multifaceted as the idea itself. Students of electoral systems, legislative institutions, public opinion–legislator linkages, identity politics, redistricting problems, and principal-agent relations continue to work at it. Agreements are hard to come by, progress is piecemeal, and closure is nowhere in sight.

Hannah Pitkin, who has given us the most familiar working definition of representation—"acting in the interest of the represented, in a manner responsive to them"[3]—has despaired of reaching philosophical agreement on the subject: "There does not seem to be any remotely satisfactory agreement on what representation is or means."[4] From an empirical perspective, Heinz Eulau, who has helped to probe "the components of responsiveness," agrees: "The puzzle of representation . . . [is] that we have representative institutions, but like the Greeks, we do not know what they are about."[5] In a recent review of several studies of representation and responsiveness, James Kuklinski and Gary Segura conclude similarly that "the more complex becomes a definition of representation, the more elusive becomes a definition of responsiveness that will accommodate them."[6] Research on representation seems destined to encompass many perspectives and to cumulate in an exceedingly incremental fashion. This study is a tiny increment in a very large and thriving enterprise.

As a contribution to the study of political representation, the Flynt-Collins case has several characteristics. First, the research takes as given the single-member-district, plurality-takes-all electoral system that governs elections to the House of Representatives.

It deliberately sidesteps macro-level questions concerning the fairness or the proportionality or the "representativeness" of the American electoral system, or of the outcomes produced by that system.[7] It assumes a structure of 435 congressional districts, one member to a district, each member representing a separate and distinguishable set of constituents. Representation, here, is a set of relationships between a House member and that member's constituents. It is also an activity. The assumption is that any activity engaged in by the representative relating to his or her constituents involves the activity of representation.

Second, the research effort centers on the individual representative and is conducted in the constituency from which that representative has been elected.

For most empirically oriented political scientists most of the time, the study of political representation focuses on voting in the legislature—on how best to explain vote patterns, both individual and collective. Representation is treated largely as a relationship between the policy preferences of a constituency and the roll-call votes of the elected legislator.[8] Typically, investigation centers on the vote choice, and the legislator's vote choice is interpreted as a representational choice. That is, it is a choice that can be studied as a response to constituency preferences.

Legislators also make another representational choice, one that is focused not on their behavior in the legislature, but on their behavior in the constituency. There the representational choice for the legislator is not "How should I vote?" but "How should I connect?" As we shall see, these two choices, when made by the same person, will impact one another and will produce behavior patterns that are related to one another. But this study is premised on the idea that making connection decisions at home can be separated analytically from making vote decisions in the legislature—and on the idea that home connections are important in their own right to the study of political representation.

The study of choices about connections is less a matter of constituency influence on the legislator—as emphasized in our empirical literature—and more a matter of the legislator's immersion in the constituency, of the legislator as part of the constituency. Home connections involve continuous interaction, and all connections count. They are more about "keeping in touch" than they are about "voting right"—though the two are related. It is harder, therefore, to isolate discrete connection choices for causal analysis than it is to separate discrete vote choices for such analysis. If it were easy, perhaps more scholars would have done it.

Since the study of home connections remains in an exploratory stage, participant observation in the constituency would seem to be an appropriate approach. And, since representing a constituency takes a lot of hard work *in* the constituency, it seems sensible for political scientists to take a look at representatives while they are actually working there. This study has been conducted largely by observing representational activity from over the shoulder of the representative and by talking with the representative about it. The study, therefore, depends one-sidedly upon the representative's words, deeds, perceptions, and interpretations. The research offers no independent account of constituency viewpoints.

Finally, this study will argue that the observable connection choices made by a representative can be summarized as the choice of a strategy of representation.

It is a constrained choice. And in order to make sense of that choice, three factors are most relevant. One is the predispositions and goals of the individual representative. Another is the context—primarily the constituency—in which the representative pursues those goals. And the third is a sequencing or developmental factor whereby prior actions may constrain choice in the present and whereby present choices may constrain future possibilities. It is expected that each of these factors can, where relevant, be found and fathomed by an observer on the scene.

The working assumption is that the choice of a strategy will produce observable patterns of representation. Conversely, the patterns observed by the researcher are assumed to be the result of a fairly deliberate strategy. The concepts of "home style" and "home strategy" are variants of the same idea. Both formulations direct research to the same place and to the same set of activities. The idea of home strategy, however, encourages us to think more directly about representation. It encourages us to separate out goals, contexts, and prior negotiations and to examine them, both separately and together, as they have shaped observable patterns of representation at home.

Goals and Contexts

All representatives are goal seekers. They have ambitions; they want to accomplish things. They make choices and work actively in pursuit of such goals as getting reelected, making good public policy, accumulating power in the legislature, and winning higher office. Representational strategies will center on such goals—playing up some, playing down others. We shall focus on each member's dominant goals. But we shall not assume that the dominance of one goal drives out all consideration of other goals. We assume, to the contrary, that all representational strategies are, of necessity, mixed strategies.

Political ambition may take root at different points in an individual's life. The earliest touches of political ambition are quite likely to occur in the context of a person's district-level relationships—and are likely to surface when an observer is immersed in the home constituency. Goals may take shape during an individual's initial decision to go into politics, as answers to the questions "Why go into politics anyway?" and "What do I want to get out of politics?" Such precongressional goals might develop from a motivation to fulfill a civic duty, to meet a self-imposed personal challenge, to savor the sociability of political involvement, to build party strength locally, or to become an ombudsman for individuals. Institutionally oriented conceptualizations may not, therefore, be sufficient for an exploration of representational activity in the political world beyond the legislature.

All representatives are context interpreters. They will make choices and take actions not in the abstract, but according to what they believe to be rational and/or appropriate in the circumstances or context in which they find themselves. And it is the goal seekers themselves who must interpret the opportunities and constraints present in that context. For members of Congress, the two most important contexts are the constituency back home and the legislative institution in Washington—along with, to a lesser extent, the political parties as they exist in both places.

Each constituency context, we assume, contains some fixed elements—such as geography, demography, the economy, and a few unshakeable issue preferences—that do not allow for interpretive latitude on the part of the representative. We also assume that the constituency context contains some variable elements—such as constituency expectations, preferences, practices, and habits—that do allow for such interpretive latitude. Therefore, we assume, each member's relationship to his or her constituents will be partly the member's responsiveness to expectations generated by the constituents and partly constituent responsiveness to expectations generated by the individual representative. The working out, over time, of a mutually satisfactory and durable fit is the object of each legislator's continuous interaction with his or her constituency.

With respect to constituency context, we assume, as discussed in *Home Style*, that each representative perceives not a single home constituency, but a set of constituencies that nest, like a series of concentric circles, within one another. The largest circle contains all the residents of the legally prescribed geographical constituency; the next smaller, the reelection constituency, contains their weak but supportive voters; and the smallest, the primary constituency, consists of their most active and most reliable supporters. Our assumption is that the constituency each member responds to is the one in his or her mind's eye. We also assume that members do not represent or connect with each of these perceived constituencies in the same way or to the same degree.

Members also cultivate supportive constituencies beyond their geographical constituency—to raise money and/or to seek higher office—to which they can be expected to respond. But, unless specifically noted, the representation of which we speak involves the home constituency.

With respect to both goal-seeking and context-interpreting, it would be unrealistic to expect a politician to lay out neatly for inspection by a visitor all the elements and interrelationships of a decision calculus or an interpretive calculus. An observer's description and analysis will, of necessity, depend heavily on retroduction—that is, treating observed comments and activities *as if* they were grounded in the pursuit of certain goals and in the interpretation of certain contexts. Throughout, an effort will be made to present evidence that gives some support to these "as if" conjectures—and, at the same time, enables other scholars to pose other possibilities.

Careers and Negotiation

Because time and sequence are such fundamental variables in this chronological study, it will be useful to think of each representative in terms of his or her career and in terms of his or her continuous negotiations with constituents. Careers and negotiations are the most important of the sequencing or developmental factors mentioned earlier, and they are crucial to the conception of representation as a long-run, over-time activity.

Out in the district, the sense of a career in progress is overwhelming. And the obligatory recitation of a representative's career milestones reveals the existence of two such careers—jointly pursued, but analytically separable. There is the career in the constituency, and there is the career in the legislative institution—and each affects the other. Our observational perch in the constituency reflects a primary interest in the career in that context. The distinction in *Home Style* between the protectionist and expansionist stages of the constituency career will be helpful in understanding each member's representational activities. The career stage at the time of observation and the story of the career to that point are among the possible constraints on present choices.

What all House members want from their constituents is support. In the short run, they want the support of a voting majority at the next election. For some members, that is all they want, or all they are free to contemplate. Others, however, may take a longer view of constituent support. For those members, reelection is a necessary, but not a sufficient, support goal. They seek a degree of constituent support that they can call upon and rely upon between elections. Their goal is what we might call durable interelection support.

These members want more from their constituents than a "yes" or "no" verdict on election day. Their calculation is not just how to win next time, but how to win consistently. They seek a support relationship that is reliable enough to guarantee them behavioral leeway between elections to pursue other goals, such as good policy or institutional power. They want a level of support that manifests itself either subjectively, in a comfortable sense of "fit," or objectively, in a stable "equilibrium" between their performance and the expectations of their constituents, especially their primary constituents.

The covering word that House members use to describe the interelection support relationship they seek is *trust*, by which they mean something akin to the benefit of the doubt, coupled with a willingness—should constituents be in doubt—to listen to the explanations of the representative. Trust, as the *Home Style* study argued at length, requires a lot of attention to the constituency, *in* the constituency, over a considerable period of time. Whether described as the achievement of a durable fit, or constituent trust, or decision-making leeway, the long-run goal for many members is to build a constituency relationship that is solid, stable, and reliable enough to be as helpful between elections as it is on election night.

The relationship between representative and constituents over the course of a constituency career can usefully be conceptualized as a negotiation. Such a negotiation at one point in time may affect—as a preexisting condition—negotiations at a later point in time, often in a path-dependent fashion. An individual's negotiating abilities and capacities (as well as goals) may also change over time and thus alter the range of strategic possibilities. The basis for negotiation is that "each has something the other wants; and each has something to offer in exchange. At the most general level, representatives want support, and they offer responsiveness. Constituents want responsiveness, and they offer support."[9] Further, in principal-agent terms, the "principal" (that is, the constituents) wants to be able regularly to monitor the state of the negotiation in order to hold its "agent" (that is, the representative) accountable.[10] Periodically, the state of the member-constituent negotiation does get monitored, and accountability is registered for all to see and evaluate, if not participate in, at election time.

While an election may be considered a one-time "test" of a representative's responsiveness, the activity of responding is continuous for the representative. When constituents vote, they are taking stock of, and passing judgment on, a whole set of activities that have been taking place for at least two years. All of the public activities and all the public contacts of House members in their home districts are acts of responsiveness. All of those actions contribute to voter assessments of the representative's responsiveness. And while students are rightfully preoccupied with the final election-day "grade" on member responsiveness, we cannot ignore the steady stream of responsive activity that contributes to that election-day judgment. Put differently, representation is an outcome, but it is not just an outcome. It is also a process. If an incumbent wins reelection, that outcome is only a punctuation point in that member's continuous, long-running efforts at representation.

Activities undertaken at home before and after election day can usefully be studied as building-block contributions to responsiveness and, therefore, as essential roots of representation. Representation is legitimized by elections, but it is redeemed by actions taken between elections. Thus, while the actions that normally command our attention are taken in Washington, if representation is our subject, we must include actions taken in the home constituency.

Every election result is provisional. The representational relationship, while tested at regular intervals, is always subject to renegotiation between elections. The process of negotiation is, then, characterized by a succession of approximations by each side to the representational preferences and expectations of the one and the performance of the other. If and when the representative achieves a comfortable fit—or a stable equilibrium—with constituents, it will be a negotiated outcome. The idea of a negotiation captures the contingent, repetitious, and developmental nature of the representational relationship—and allows for the possibility that member strategies might change over time. The idea also allows for the appearance of historically constrained, path-dependent strategies.

Constituents, we assume, have some elementary notion, or can develop some notion, of what good or satisfactory representation looks like. In the beginning, constituents' judgments about good representation and about their own representative will be minimally informed and maximally unstable. Name recognition and basic qualifications will suffice. The representative will—through a mixture of responsiveness and independence, promise and performance—"set a mark" or "make an impression" that constituency elites, at least, will recognize and characterize.[11] After repeated interaction, constituency expectations and judgments become more informed, more differentiated, and more stable. Over time, the early, tentative mark, or impression, develops into a fuller, more recognizable pattern of activity—that is, into a reputation.[12]

A favorable reputation will cut the costs, for constituents, of acquiring new information and will aid in the development of trust. And with trust can come the achievement of durable interelection support, increased legislative leeway, and an ever more recognizable representational pattern. An equilibrium may be established in which a certain degree of member independence is recognized, accepted, and valued by a preponderance of constituents. In cases of unusual longevity of the representative, constituents may stop taking in new information altogether and instead make a standing commitment based on incumbent reputation and constituent trust.[13] In sum, reputation, trust, and leeway are career-related phenomena. All must be negotiated over time.

Representation as Process

Combining the discussion of goals and contexts with the discussion of sequential activities involving careers and negotiation leads us, finally, to think of the phenomenon of representation as a process. And that conceptualization, in turn, requires that representation be studied over time. That is the logic that emerges from the introduction of such ideas as multiple goals, changing contexts, building connections, developing career sequences, continuous responsiveness, continuous negotiation, durable fits, increasing leeway, solidifying a reputation, and winning trust.

Representation is not only a political process, it is a distinctive political process. It is related to the electoral process, but it is not the same as the electoral process. It is related to the legislative process, but it is not the same as the legislative process. Representational strategy is related to campaign strategy in running for Congress, and it is related to voting strategy inside Congress. But it is not identical to campaign strategy or to voting strategy. As conceptualized in this study, representation is an autonomous process.

Legislation and representation, our textbooks tell us, are two parts of a single job. Indeed, the process of representation, as it is described in this book, has many similarities to the legislative process—as that process has been described in our research. Both are slow moving, incremental, repetitious, and continuous negotiating processes that occur under conditions of uncertainty. Both processes are punctuated, on occasion, by votes—roll calls in Congress and election results in the districts—that provide some temporary finality. Students of both processes have used these punctuating votes to characterize or to measure legislative and/or representational outcomes.

It has been axiomatic, however, for students of the legislative process to probe deeply, and in detail, the lengthy and complex building-block negotiations that lie behind successful performance of the legislative side of the job. Many such students have gone to Washington to have a firsthand look at this process, and their case studies of "how a bill becomes a law" have become foundation stones of congressional research. Fewer students of representation, on the other hand, have thought it important to dig into or trace the building-block negotiations that lie behind and lead up to successful performance of the representational side of the job. Fewer still have gone to the districts to examine firsthand the myriad member-constituency connections that the representational part of the job requires.

Despite the links between the two sides of a representative's job and the commonalities of the two processes, therefore, we do not have an equivalent case study literature on "how an elected official connects with a constituency." The following study might be read as an invitation to think about the absence of such a literature and about the potential contribution it might make to the larger study of political representation.

CHAPTER TWO

Jack Flynt, 1970–1972

A Person-Intensive Strategy

Individual and Goals

When I arrived in Georgia in October 1970, Jack Flynt was fifty-six years old, in his sixteenth year in Congress and his twenty-fourth consecutive year in elective office. Born, raised, and still residing at that time in Griffin, Georgia, Flynt was a graduate of the private Woodward Academy, the University of Georgia, and the George Washington University Law School. His major career milestones included service as an army officer in World War II, for which he was decorated with a Bronze Star; appointment as assistant district attorney for northern Georgia in 1939 (a post to which he returned after the war); election at age thirty-one to one term (1947–48) in the Georgia House of Representatives from his home county; election (in 1948 and 1952) to two terms as solicitor general (prosecuting attorney) for the four-county Griffin Judicial Circuit; election to the U.S. House of Representatives in 1954 and reelection from 1956 to 1978; and appointment to the House Committee on Appropriations in 1962. He was a career politician, in the sense that all of his civilian jobs had been connected with the political arena. His political career had been one unbroken electoral success.

Flynt grew up in a locally rooted, locally prominent, and successful political family—a sixth-generation Georgian on both sides of his family. In that context, he was attracted early to politics. His grandfather had been a state senator. His father was a successful lawyer and farmer—"on 1,500 acres of the best farm land in the county"—who had been elected to two terms as state court judge, four terms in the Georgia house, and three terms in the state senate, where he became senate president and, in the words of his admiring son, "the patron saint of Georgia agriculture." Flynt made certain that I visited the local monuments to his father's service. Given this political genealogy, it seemed natural that the son would follow the family footsteps into politics. And he never indicated otherwise.

When Jack Flynt Jr. decided to run for office, he had two goals, one more immediate, one more long-run. First, he wanted to meet the personal challenge of his father's only failure. "My father ran for Congress when I was eight years old, and he lost. I suppose that's the reason why I always wanted to go to Congress." Second, he wanted to enjoy the personal involvements of political life. When I met Flynt, he had accomplished the first goal and was still being motivated primarily by the second one.

As a local boy, raised in a political family, Flynt imbibed the supreme importance of personal relationships in politics. His reminiscences focused on the importance of making and preserving these personal relationships. "I had been tempted to run for Congress [earlier]," he said. "But [incumbent congressman] Sid Camp was a dear friend of mine and a very dear friend of my father's, and so I couldn't do it." And Camp, said Flynt, "was instrumental, to say the least" in getting him his first job, one "in which . . . I acquired a good reputation as a trial lawyer and made friends that have been a great help to me ever since." Indeed, in 1954 he was elected president of the Georgia State Bar Association.

More than any politician I had ever met, Flynt placed our relationship on personal terms. In 1970 he and his wife, Patty, drove forty miles to meet my first Saturday evening flight. He did the same thing in 1972, and she did it again in 1976. I enjoyed the hospitality of their home during that first four-day trip, and again for five days in 1972. During my first two visits, the congressman also arranged for me to join him in private dinner or luncheon conversations with his political friends—the CEO of a large textile company, a former governor of Georgia, a former Washington staff member, and his own state senator—not to mention meals with his wife, son, and daughter. His personal attentiveness to me undergirded my sense that he genuinely enjoyed people—visiting with them, learning about them, helping them. And it fortified my conclusion that his initial attraction to politics had rested heavily on the special pleasure he derived from its personal connections. The importance he placed on my meeting people also suggested the value of such connections for him.

If politics was primarily about people, then it made sense that representation was, for Flynt, primarily a matter of personal relationships with his constituents. That view, I believe, had propelled him to continuous electoral success.

In his first race, for the Georgia House of Representatives, he was the local boy running in a single-county constituency of about 6,000 voters. A hands-on, friends-and-neighbors campaign was virtually dictated by that context. When he next ran for solicitor, he added three nearby rural counties and 6,000 more voters—and folded a chunk of them into his strongly supportive primary and reelection constituencies. By the time he ran for Congress, in a primary that attracted 56,373 voters, a strategy of representation that centered on his local-boy, friends-and-neighbors, person-to-person relationships had been well established. Every incentive moved him, in path-dependent fashion, to keep the strategy with which he had begun. And there is every evidence that this strategy—initially successful in a small, homogeneous electorate and then applied to ever-larger electorates—was personally satisfying to him in meeting his goal of involvement in the political community.

Context

Flynt's constituency relationships developed, however, within a very distinctive context of time and place, a time of transition in the South. A good deal of excellent research has been done on the transition from the "Old South" to the "New South"—most helpfully, for my purposes, by Earl Black and Merle Black in their splendid book, *Politics and Society in the South*.[1] Jack Flynt's thirty-two-year political career spanned this time of transition. His successful strategy of representation took root and thrived in the context of the Old South. It came under challenge, however, in the context of the New South.

Every micro-level representational story is partly about the representative and partly about the constituency. The story of Flynt's early success and his later challenge takes place in the context of his changing district: his original district (1954–64), his transitional district (1966–70), and his new district (1972–76).

Flynt's original district—or geographical constituency—consisted of fifteen rural and small-town counties south and west of Atlanta

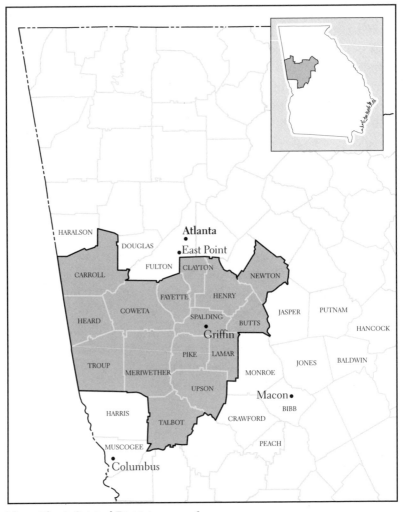

Map 1. Flynt's Original District, 1954–1964
(Georgia's Fourth Congressional District)

(see map 1), and that is where he adopted and perfected his basic
representational strategy. The counties ranged in population from
7,000 to 50,000, with the median county population at 20,000. Their
total population in 1954 was 298,000. His home county (Spalding),
the third most populous, was located near the geographical center of
the district. Census figures in 1960 described it as 92 percent rural,
with a high 65 percent of the workforce holding blue-collar jobs.[2]
The district's dominant economic interest was textiles, followed by
farming and some light metal and food-processing industries. Sixty-
nine percent of the population was white and 31 percent was black.

It was a one-party, Democratic district in which the only meaning-ful election contests occurred in the Democratic primary. The only serious primary contest Flynt ever had in this district was his initial 1954 victory. In a three-way contest, he won 49 percent of the vote and carried twelve of the fifteen counties.[3] He explained that victory as a personal one. Speaking of his nearest competitor (with 31 per-cent of the vote), he said, "He was attractive, a good friend, a state senator, and had a fine background. But he was inclined to be a bit lazy, and not as aggressive a campaigner as I was. *In philosophy we were about the same"* (emphasis added). This initial victory thus reinforced Flynt's person-oriented approach to politics. For the next five elections, he ran essentially unopposed.

In 1964 the Supreme Court intervened with its one person/one vote decision, and Flynt was redistricted into his transitional district, with a slightly larger population of 323,000 and a voting electorate that had nearly doubled to 120,000 (see map 2). He now represented a geographical constituency of sixteen counties, having traded two small counties for two other equally small ones and picking up one large county (Bibb) that contained his first real city, Macon (popu-lation 122,000). Otherwise, the demographics were little changed. The black population, for example, dropped from 31 to 27 percent. With Macon came Flynt's first taste of two-party politics. In 1966 he faced his first general election contest—against Macon's Republican state representative and Republican state chairman, a "quality chal-lenger." Flynt won that contest with 68 percent of the vote, even carrying the home county (Bibb) of his opponent. For the next two elections, he ran unopposed. (His new district will be discussed in Chapter 3.)

Because all of my visits with Flynt came during campaign time, it is important to state my view that campaigning and representing are separable but interrelated processes. When we study campaigning, we also study representation. As I have argued at length elsewhere, "Campaigns connect politicians and citizens, and make possible the accountability of politicians to citizens that representative govern-ment requires. In short, no campaigns, no connections; no connec-tions, no accountability; no accountability, no representative govern-ment."[4] If we think of representation as a process, then campaigning for Congress is as central a representational activity as voting in Congress. Indeed, it was the campaign context that prompted Ed-mund Burke's classic discussion of political representation. As indi-

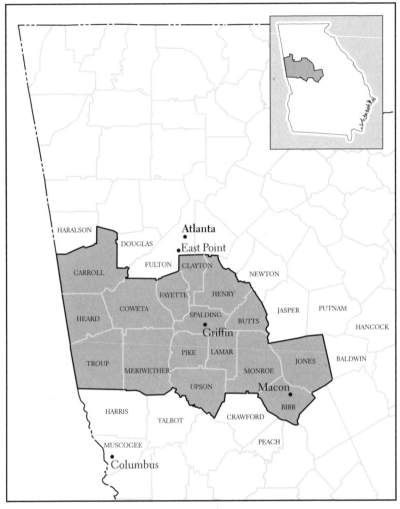

Map 2. Flynt's Transitional District, 1966–1970
(Georgia's Sixth Congressional District)

cated earlier, there is a lot more to representation than campaigning.
But students of representation who do not study campaigning de-
prive themselves of some critical leverage in understanding the negotiating dynamics endemic to their subject.

1970, Day One: Personal Connections

We began my first day in the district by driving to a Baptist church in
Macon, where Congressman Flynt spoke briefly during Sunday services to a large congregation (over 1,000) of, in his words, "indepen-

dent businessmen, people who work at Warner Robins air base—middle class, very conservative, and part of my greatest strength." It went without saying that this congregation was white, as all his gatherings would be throughout this visit.

We spent the afternoon dropping in, unannounced, on a succession of Flynt's personal acquaintances, the first at one o'clock in Macon and the last at six o'clock back home in Griffin. These two endpoint visits were with the topmost officials of two textile companies: in Macon, with the CEO of the largest company (5,000 employees) in Flynt's district, and in Griffin, with the CEO of the largest company (2,000 employees) in his home county. In between, we visited in the homes of a Macon banker, a Mercer University administrator, and the owner of a Monroe County cotton mill. Twice, he stopped the car to greet—"Hey, how you doin'?"—individuals he spotted as we drove along.

During these five home visits, conversation centered on families, churches, flowers, trees, and football loyalties. With election day only two days away, there was an occasional sprinkling of political opinion. But Flynt had no opposition, and politics was a very minor note. Mostly there was an easygoing, familiar, reinforcing exchange of small talk and pleasantries. In the process, however, there were implicit exchanges of mutual regard and implicit confirmation of the constituents' established pattern of support and of the congressman's established pattern of responsiveness. Only once did politics break the surface. Before sitting down to dinner in the home of Griffin's textile company president, Flynt took his constituent aside and relayed "the word" on a relevant tax problem as conveyed to him "personally" by "Chairman [Wilbur] Mills" of the House Ways and Means Committee.

During the trip to and from Macon, our "travel talk" centered on the district's two major economic interests—agriculture and textiles. Here, too, the strong impression was one of a comfortable, "me-in-the-constituency" relationship. Riding to Macon through the rural countryside, Flynt kept up a running commentary on various types of farming—row-cropping for cotton, livestock management for dairying, harvesting practices for peaches and pecans—displaying a fund of agricultural knowledge. He revealed that he himself owned a 300-acre farm in an adjacent county, with "livestock and a little hay and corn for feed." On a tour of his thirty-four-acre wooded home site that evening, he enthusiastically identified twenty-three varieties of trees. He seemed to have an attachment to the land that would stand him in good stead with the district's farmers.

On the way back from Macon, our visits with the various textile-connected individuals spurred talk of that industry. There was local concern about increased foreign competition, but for now, "the mills are running at full capacity. [And] anyone who wants a job and is willing to work can find one in the Sixth District." The importance of the textile industry to Flynt and to the district was obvious. As he put it later, "The thing that ties the district together is the textile industry and the dependence of the people of the district—employer and employee—on the textile industry. If I were hostile to the textile industry, it would be fatal. But that could never happen, because I feel so close to the textile industry." Given the fact that trade unions in the textile industry were notoriously weak and difficult to organize in the South, the congressman faced little or no countervailing union presence in his district.[5] At first glance he seemed to have inherited—and/or established—solid personal attachments to the dominant interests of the district.

In the evening, when I asked how the day had gone for him, Flynt said simply, "There were 200,000 people I didn't see." He added, "In Georgia, only a person-to-person campaign will work." That statement revealed his controlling perception of constituency politics and his basic choice as a representative—to have some kind of personal connection with as many constituents as possible.

As he saw it, his personal connections had two aspects: personal contact and personal service. Personal contact was the more visible of the two activities, but personal service was implicit in every contact and available to every constituent. Taken together, they defined a strategy of personal accessibility. Flynt wanted to be accessible, and he wanted to have the reputation for being accessible. As he put it the next day, "I could vote conservative or liberal on any piece of legislation, and most of the people of my district wouldn't care a bit—so long as they know I'll help them when they come to me with a problem. The main image they have [of me] is that if they come to me for help, I'll do everything I can to help them. Another part of the image I like to think I have is that they can talk to me, and that if they are talking, they feel that I am listening to them, listening to what they have to say. Some people have the ability to make people feel that way and some don't."

It was an overwhelmingly person-intensive strategy, as befitted someone who had been attracted to politics by its people-oriented opportunities for sociability and service. For Jack Flynt, personal accessibility was the essence of good representation. He believed that the steady practice of it had won him a favorable reputation among his constituents, their durable interelection support, and, therefore, a measurable degree of operating leeway in Washington.[6]

1970, Day Two: Upson County Elites

Politically, Jack Flynt conceptualized and cataloged his district as a collection of counties—some smaller or larger than others, some more or less supportive than others, some more or less factionalized than others, some that he had represented a longer or shorter time than others. One of his pet pastimes was encouraging county historians in the district to write histories of their counties—and encouraging his own staffers to research both the origins of each county's name and the backgrounds of its families.

Earl Black and Merle Black characterize rural politics in the Old South as centering around the "county seat elites," where political and economic influence were blended and concentrated.[7] For Flynt, the county seat elites made up the core of his primary constituency— the people whose support he most needed, most wanted, and most assiduously cultivated. They were the essential cue givers of constituency politics, the individuals who provided the "elite certification" of a candidate's qualifications that is so essential to early political success.[8] In my three visits to Georgia, we visited seven different county seats, where the congressman gave his personal attention to the leading citizens who worked and lived there.

We spent my second day in 1970 visiting with people in and around Thomaston, the county seat of Upson County, at the southern rim of the district. On the way down, however, we stopped off at Gunnells and Sons, a general store in Pike County. It was my first visit to one of these local communication centers, which dotted the rural areas beyond Main Street and had long been favorite Flynt stops on the personal contact trail. "When I was out campaigning," he reminisced, "I would stop in a country store. I would buy some cheese and canned salmon or sardines and some crackers. And I would share with whomever was there—and buy more if need be. Do you know that a man who eats salmon and crackers with you will vote for you? And if a man takes a bite of your chewing tobacco—or, better still, if he gives you a bite of his chewing tobacco—he'll not only vote for you, he'll fight for you."

At the Gunnells store, the proprietor recalled their longtime connections. "Jack used to stop by when he was solicitor. And I would tell him that he ought to run for Congress. When I heard on the radio that [incumbent] Sid Camp had died, I called Jack on the phone at five o'clock in the morning. I told him, 'You don't have any excuse for not running now, Jack.'" The congressman, giving full credit to Howell Gunnells for being first with the news, completed the story of how he chased the registrar "all over Georgia" and "qualified" even before Camp's funeral.

In every one of my visits, there would be at least one stop at a country store. This network of contacts gave me a different and broader view of Flynt's constituents than the one I had gotten earlier from the big yards and well-appointed family rooms we visited on the way home from Macon—or the view I was about to get from the county seat elite in Upson County. The country store proprietors were an important segment of Flynt's active primary constituency, and their customers made up a large part of his wider reelection constituency. These individuals, too, thought of Jack Flynt in terms of their personal contact with him.

Upson County (population 23,500), as Flynt saw it, was "one of the most Democratic of my counties, and more industrialized than some because of the [textile] mills. I've carried it by 94 percent on occasion. People work together here, very well—no factions." Upson County votes (like those of Pike County) had helped elect him solicitor in 1948, and he had represented those voters ever since. Several times during the day's palaver, Flynt signaled his attachment by saying, "This is my county, you know." Recalling a suggestion during the 1964 redistricting that Upson be removed from his district, he added, "Someone asked me, 'What would you do if that happened?' I said, 'I'd move to Thomaston.' And I didn't hesitate a bit, did I, not a bit."[9] The more palpable was his sense of community on any occasion, the more he thrived personally and politically.

On Thomaston's main street, he visited the insurance company, the newspaper office, and the office equipment store and exchanged greetings with people in between. On the street, everyone seemed to recognize him. We lunched in the local tearoom with the editor of the paper, who had helped write Flynt's campaign ads in his 1966 campaign. He commented at lunch, "There are 115,000 voters in the

Sixth District, and Jack knows them all. And they know him. I don't see how you can succeed in politics in any other way. You have to know the people. Maybe you can get away with it once on some other basis, but not the second time. You've got to get out in the street and meet people." After lunch, the congressman walked through the county courthouse, "meeting and greeting" the public officials and employees, along with the members of the sitting grand jury.

In the afternoon, in the company of the chairman of the county commissioners, the county superintendent of public works, and the county's largest peach grower, we drove to the proposed site of a dam on the scenic Flint River. Flynt had overcome opposition in Congress to secure an appropriation to fund the initial construction efforts, and there was a lot of shared pleasure at this joint accomplishment. For the congressman, it was a chance to underscore his clout—as a member of the Appropriations Committee—in getting something tangible and beneficial for his constituents.

The ride exposed me to Flynt's amazing appetite—and memory— for people, time, and place. "Didn't George Smith build that house?" "Whose cannery is that—Hubert's?" "Isn't this old Route 74?" "Doesn't Alabama Road come out over there?" "That's old Bert Williams's house, isn't it?" "Wasn't Sassie his sister?" "Oh, sister-in-law." "Wasn't the house built in 1945—or was it 1946?" And, at the site, "Do you know what the Indian name for the river was? And do you know what it meant? 'River with beds of flint.'" "Do you know that this river formed the boundary of the Creeks' land?" "Do you know that everywhere the Indian trails crossed in this area, there is a major highway intersection today?" "Do you know that somewhere in this valley, there's a place that is the southernmost location of trailing arbutus and the northernmost location of Spanish moss? The two plants meet." The depth of his immersion in the detail of the area was remarkable. And I soon learned that this process of sorting, filing, cataloging, and rehearsing the details of his district was never-ending. Details were the essential "stuff" of his quotidian person-to-person connections.

On the way back to town, we detoured so that the congressman could inspect—in person and with appropriate admiration—first, the newly mounted deer's head at the commissioner's home, then the new stone patio at the superintendent's home, and, finally, the spring-fed drinking water at the peach grower's home. In town, we stopped at the county courthouse to pick up some turnip greens someone had left for him and then returned to the newspaper office, where the editor gave him an inscribed copy of the new *History of Upson County*. When Flynt spied a picture of the editor's four children, he proceeded to name and inquire about each one. We dropped in on a law office and went, finally, to talk with the president of the bank.

The bank president made a comment similar to that of the editor, but it carried a message. "Jack, things are changing," he said. "You don't want to spend all your time with people like me. You want to get out in the stores, the filling stations, and the barber shops—where the people are. We are establishment and a lot of people are against the establishment now. I know I don't have to tell you, but there are a lot of young people just itching to take over your job. So you listen to what I say, because we want you to be the chairman of the [House] Appropriations Committee." Flynt replied firmly, "That's what I do now." He remembered the message sufficiently to report it that evening to his wife—with a chuckle, but without comment. I noted it, however, as evidence of a protectionist career stage—that he was still campaigning and representing just the way he always had. And I noted, too, that the county elites clearly recognized their investment in that career.

1970, Day Three: Henry County Elites

We spent election day, 1970, in the company of another set of county seat elites—in the town of McDonough in Henry County (population 23,700). Here, on the northern rim of the district, far from Upson County, there was a palpable portent of change. In Flynt's eyes, Henry was a once-thriving cotton-producing county that had been reduced to a single cotton gin and was preparing itself for the impact of the southward-moving Atlanta metropolis. The congressman began the day by participating in a public meeting at the courthouse with the county board of commissioners to discuss the federal/state/local financing of new water and sewer projects. Afterward, he went to lunch with several people from the meeting.

Riding to lunch with two commissioners, Flynt again reached back in time to underscore his personal identification with the county. "Did you know," he said, "that a Henry County man saved my grandfather in the Civil War? In the Battle of Sharpsburg, my grandfather was badly wounded, and Sergeant Kelly from Kellytown picked him up and carried him off the field—just a bloody uniform with pieces of bone sticking out. An orderly stopped him and said, 'What are you doing carrying that corpse?' Sergeant Kelly said, 'That's no corpse, that's Captain Flynt. And so long as there's a spark of life in him, I'm going to do my best to save him!' He did, and my grandfather lived. My roots go deep in Henry County." In the Old South, Earl Black and Merle Black tell us, politics was often driven by shared memories of the Civil War.[10] And those memories were carried, say the authors, by the generation of southerners who came of voting age before World War II—Jack Flynt's generation. Flynt was a history buff, and he often invoked the Civil War to build links to various constituents.

In the afternoon, the congressman "beat the bushes" and swapped bits of local lore along the main street—with a Chevrolet dealer, a doctor, a hardware store owner, a post office manager, and the county historian. He called at the home of a black funeral director, but no one was there. Everyone he met that day was invited to come to his home that evening to watch the election returns.

On the way home, Flynt alluded frequently to elements of his personal connections pattern. He summed up the visit this way: "If I had been campaigning hard, I would not have stopped at any one place more than one minute, and no more than ten seconds at most places. And I would have seen 800 people." He then extracted a personal contact rule of thumb from the visit. "Did you see that woman back in the post office? She had never seen me before, but she called me 'Jack.' That's the way people think of me. No person will ever vote against you if he is on a first-name basis with you. Did you know that?" And he told a story that ended in more person-to-person advice. "If you want someone to support you, don't do him a favor. Let him help you. That's human nature. You saw that sign I have over our kitchen sink—'Why are you mad at me? I haven't done you any favors.'"

He also revealed the crosscutting effects of his person-intensive representational strategy. "I should turn here and go down to Locust Grove, but I haven't the time. If I went there, there are about a dozen people I would have to see. Two of them are very close to me, much closer than the others. But if I went to see those two and didn't go to see the other ten, word would get around and I would lose Locust Grove in the next election. That's how it is." Flynt's established set of personal connections had become constraining as well as liberating. His prior activity in negotiating personal contacts had established boundaries that restricted his representational choices in the present. It was not the last time that I watched him make such path-dependent negotiating decisions.

Near the end of our drive home, we stopped by a dusty field where the congressman's son, his farm manager/aide, and eight or ten other hunters were warming themselves with a little whiskey after a cold afternoon spent shooting doves. There he shared drinks and hunting jokes.

> Flynt: How come you shot that bird when he was still running along the ground?
> Hunter: I didn't shoot him while he was running; I waited till he stopped.

That evening, watching the election returns, the aide said, "Jack, those men standing by the road this afternoon would fight, die, and go to hell for you, and you know it." "Yes," was the reply, "I know it—all of them." Flynt's love of hunting and his knowledge of guns provided strong connective tissue with a broad base of his supporters.[11]

Half of the fifteen to twenty guests who came to watch the election returns that evening had been collected during the day. They came in markedly informal attire. Only one came with a suit and tie. One came in his hunting clothes; most wore open shirts or sweatshirts. They milled around, had a drink or two, gossiped, and left early—as soon as Jimmy Carter's gubernatorial victory was assured. The congressman himself began the evening in his stocking feet and soon was walking around barefoot, chewing tobacco, spitting into a paper cup, and pausing now and then to read a couple of pages in his recently acquired *History of Upson County*, which lay open on the back of a chair.

During my first three days with Jack Flynt, I observed a representational relationship that had been long in the making. A person-intensive strategy takes a lot of time and requires continuous incremental updating and reinforcing. I could not tell, of course, which had come first, Flynt's strategic preferences or constituency expectations—or how much, therefore, he had felt constrained by preexisting conditions in the beginning. By the time I got there, however, the requisite incremental negotiations had been completed, his support base was sturdy, and his continued political success seemed assured.

Though he had no formal campaign, he was still campaigning—a never-ending activity, in his view. "I'm not campaigning for this election," he said. "I'm campaigning for the next election." And that was his reputation. As one Lamar County shopkeeper said to him, "Jack, when you were solicitor, you used to be around here all the time. Now, I swear, you get around to see us even more. I don't know how you do it." Students of American politics in the 1990s—drawn to the study of political campaigns by the dominance of fund-raising—may believe that they have discovered "the permanent campaign." Far from it! Jack Flynt conducted a permanent campaign, one in which the central activity was not relentless fund-raising, but relentless personal networking.

He was certainly campaigning in pursuit of his short-run reelection goal. But he had another goal—to maintain the reliable set of constituency relationships that he had negotiated over a considerable period of time. He was pursuing the goal of durable interelection support. His permanent campaign was designed to protect the comfortable fit—the negotiated equilibrium—between his performance and the expectations of the active elements of his constituency. That relationship had already given him valued leeway inside the legislative institution. Everything I observed could be understood as evidence of the continuing execution of a solidly grounded and carefully negotiated representational relationship by a politician now in the protectionist stage of his constituency career.

Personal Service

In all of Flynt's personal contacts, the idea of personal service was implicit. The congressman had a small district staff (two people in Griffin, one in Macon) whose time was devoted almost wholly to casework—helping individuals who had problems with the government. Handling Vietnam servicemen's requests, Social Security matters, veteran's benefits, passport applications, immigration hardships, service academy applications, and other constituent problems, the staffers even made "house calls" to the ill and the elderly.[12] But Flynt did not take them with him when he traveled, and the staff never spoke publicly on his behalf. "It wouldn't work. People want to see me—the congressman."

The emphasis was on *personal* service. Flynt picked up casework as he went along. Once in a general store and once in a hardware store, he learned about young men who wanted to apply to the Air

Force Academy. In each case, the congressman—who was well positioned as a congressional member of the academy's Board of Visitors—picked up the store's phone, called his district office, gave his staffers the details, and told them to make sure the young man received encouragement along with the proper materials. In the same spirit of personal, individualized service, *every* letter that originated in either district office was sent directly to Washington so that Flynt could sign it himself along with the other outgoing mail and add whatever personal salutation or notation he wished.

Our 1972 visit to Butts County (population 10,600) brought lavish praise from a county official for the district staff's help in expediting a passport. That prompted Flynt to generalize about its political significance for him. "David," he said, "is one of my strongest supporters. My strong supporters don't give a damn how I vote. They know me and trust me. David couldn't say enough about the office for speeding up that passport application. He's clerk at the Superior Court. People come to him, and he knows what something like that means to a person. He could care less how I vote in Congress." The last statement, of course, was not true. Flynt's representational relationship with his strong supporters depended on the validity of his perception that "they know me and trust me." And crucial to that perception was his personal service and his reputation for the same.

Representative and constituent had, over time, come to see personal service as a necessary, if not primary, element of good representation. And the representative's negotiated reputation in that respect seemed solid. He liked to quote an old friend who said that "Jack Flynt loves his service to his constituents so much he ought to serve pro bono."

Personal service provides a potential link with everyone within a representative's geographical constituency. Flynt was especially pleased when he was introduced as being "comfortable with blue serge and blue denim, with rich folks and po' folks." For some of his constituents, however, personal service was about all they could hope for by way of a representational connection. Only twice during my first two visits did he make an effort to talk with a black constituent. One was the undertaker we missed, and the other was a Griffin city councilman and owner of a dry-cleaning business with whom we visited at his store. To the degree that the congressman's representational relationships and reputation depended on repeated personal contact, only white people were well represented. But to the degree that his relationships and reputation depended also on personal service, Flynt believed that individual black constituents, too, had reason to think of him as their representative.

Driving away from the dry-cleaning establishment, I asked him whether he attended functions in the black community. "I do," he answered, "and they ask me in ways that won't embarrass me, or them. I went to dedicate the new wing of a nursing home here in Griffin. Afterwards, they wanted to pay me an honorarium. I said I didn't want it, that I was their congressman, that I came because I wanted to, and that when they put on another wing, if they wanted me, I'd come back and dedicate it, too." He added, "The black people who know me know I will help them with their problems. All things being equal, I will work harder to help a black person than a white person on an individual case." He was telling me that when it came to requests for personal service, he was as obliging—formally, privately, and without publicity—to blacks as he was to whites.

Jack Flynt was a segregationist. Within that context, however, he prided himself on his scrupulous efforts at equal and dignified treatment of all individual black constituents. And he believed that his behavior toward his black constituents had won him some political support. "As far as people around here are concerned," he said, "I am [as] tolerant and fair on racial matters as anyone."

As evidence, he often cited his 1954 congressional primary contest.

When I first ran for Congress, my opponents were developing the thought that I couldn't get the black vote, that they could beat me in that way. . . . Some leaders supporting another candidate came down from Atlanta, and they made the mistake of holding their meeting in my hometown. At the meeting, when the chairman got up and asked how [black] people felt about me, no one spoke up. Finally, one man said, "I don't know about the rest of you, but I'm going to vote for Mr. Jack. . . . When we speak to him, he listens to us. I know that he was the first solicitor to convict a white man of raping a Negro woman, and I know that he was the first solicitor to convict a white man of murdering a Negro man. . . . Furthermore, when he talks to us in the courtroom, he uses the same tone of voice he uses when he talks to a white man." For him, this last thing was the clincher, the most important of all. And I believe it is, too. I was ahead of my time.

The black vote, Flynt believed, contributed to the size of his victory margin in that key race.

He also believed that the personal relationships he had fostered in the black community helped contribute to the absence of overt racial conflict in his district. Referring to a leading black woman in Griffin, he said,

> That woman is as liberal as Shirley Chisholm. But she'll vote for me come hell or high water, because I'm honest with her. And I have moderated my views. I'm more moderate than I used to be. In some cases [funding for the National Endowments for the Arts and Humanities], I've admitted that I was just plain wrong. . . . My constituents have changed, too. And I like to think they have changed because I have changed. We've never had—let me knock on wood—any racial strife in my district. We've had racial tension, but not racial strife. I like to think it's because I have stepped in to head it off. On a number of occasions, I have done that and the situation has cooled off.

When I asked for an example, Flynt said he had once persuaded some black people in Griffin to moderate their demands before the city council.

Since all his examples of personal interaction with black constituents applied to his hometown of Griffin, I concluded that while his personal relationships in Griffin were—within the confines of a segregated system—relatively amicable, the congressman's experience with his black constituents was limited mostly to that locale. This conclusion about lack of outreach was strengthened when, after a 1972 sesquicentennial celebration speech to a large, racially mixed outdoor crowd in neighboring Pike County—which he had represented since 1949—only white people came up to talk with him personally. When I noted this fact, he said, "I was surprised, very frankly, that more [black people] did not come up afterward. But they don't know me as well in Pike County as they do in Spalding County."

The constituents on whom a supportive response to his person-intensive representational strategy depended were white. Among the white electorate, Flynt's lifelong association, his accessibility, and his presentation of self as being at one with them had given him a durable cushion of interelection support. His fit with the people he touched—the equilibrium between their expectations and his performance—was so well balanced and so well matched that the representative and his district seemed ideally suited to one another.

Policy Connections

The process of representation is only partly about making personal connections. It is also about making policy connections. Observation in eighteen constituencies for the *Home Style* study produced the conclusion—without any estimates of relative frequency—that "the most common and the most easily recognizable of all presentational styles [were] a style heavily weighted toward the cultivation of personal relationships [and] a style heavily weighted toward the discussion of policy issues." That same distinction proved equally helpful in a later study of ten U.S. senators.[13]

When I asked Jack Flynt which type of connection was most important to him, he answered, "Both." "A friend of mine who knows a lot about politics says that unless you went completely wild on the issues, it doesn't matter how you vote—that personal contact is more important. I wouldn't go quite that far. I think it takes both." Doubtless his conclusion is accurate. All representatives will adopt a mixture of styles consisting of some personal goals leading to personal connections and some policy goals leading to policy connections. The inference I drew from observing Flynt's behavior, however, was that he had long since made a definite choice in favor of the former.

It is hard to make an airtight case that Flynt deliberately chose the person-intensive, personal accessibility representational strategy described here. He certainly behaved as if he had. The case is strengthened, however, if he behaved as if he had deliberately *rejected* the most prominent alternative strategy, a policy-intensive, policy advocacy representational style. And from everything I observed, that is exactly what he had done. Neither outside nor inside Congress was he a formulator or an articulator or a mobilizer or a leading decision maker in the realm of public policy. He never spoke of a bill, an amendment, or an initiative he was especially proud of. Flynt did not get into politics to make good public policy, and it was never a prominent goal of his. He had strong policy preferences, but—with the single exception of the Vietnam War—he did not express or elaborate them unless he had to, and then he did so only in generalities.

Nevertheless, the success of Flynt's personal connections with his constituents can only be understood in the context of his policy connections. He and three-quarters of his constituents shared a basic agreement on social and fiscal conservatism. It was their agreement on fiscal conservatism that was invoked whenever policy matters were raised during our travels. But the linchpin of this conservative consensus was the agreement on policies involving race.

Policy Context and Race

Had Jack Flynt not been in very basic agreement with his constituency—both primary and reelection—on the preservation of racial segregation and of white economic and political dominance, his constituents would not have "liked" him or "known" him or "supported" him or "trusted" him. In a 1954 statewide referendum, his district voted 62 percent—by majorities in fourteen out of fifteen counties—in support of maintaining segregated schools.[14] And in the presidential election of 1968, the avowedly segregationist candidate, George Wallace, carried all fifteen counties over both major party candidates. No opponent of Flynt's—Democrat or Republican—ever challenged him on any of his race-based policy stands.

On the campaign trail, the congressman did not have to express opinions on the subject. Everyone knew what they were, and no one challenged him to state them out loud. When called upon in Congress to take a position on civil rights legislation, however, he left no doubt about his prosegregationist opinions. He (like all but three southern House members) signed the Southern Manifesto in protest against the Supreme Court's desegregation decision in *Brown v. Board of Education*. He voted against the Civil Rights Act of 1964 and the Voting Rights Act of 1965. But he rarely, if ever, spoke directly about civil rights on the House floor. During a debate on civil rights in 1960, he wrote into the *Congressional Record* his opinion that "never in the history of this country has there been such an effort made to perpetuate a bad and evil thing as has been undertaken since May 17, 1954, to implement the decision of the Supreme Court in the school cases."[15]

In 1970 Flynt mentioned his civil rights votes to me twice. "I don't promise [black constituents] things I know I can't deliver," he said. "If I did that, I would get myself in a bind from which I could never extricate myself. I don't promise so-called civil rights bills which, to my mind, are the cause of much of the permissiveness and rioting we have today." And, reflecting on our visit with the black city councilman at his dry-cleaning establishment, he commented, "My Negro friends this morning don't get mad at me. They don't expect me to vote for those crazy civil rights bills, and they completely forgive me for my civil rights votes." Whatever his rationale, Flynt's policy preferences were never in doubt.

My working assumption was that the few politically active black people in his district were still accommodating to what Earl Black and Merle Black describe as "the reality" and "the finality" of "white power," and, further, that the great bulk of his black constituents were not yet politically active.[16] In 1958, for example, black constituents made up 31 percent of the district population, but only 15 percent of its registered voters, while white constituents made up 69 percent of the population and 85 percent of the registered voters.[17]

Though we have no racial breakdown of actual voters, it seems likely that the black influence at the polls was smaller still, since these constituents had no alternative but to acquiesce in the world in which Jack Flynt had cut his political teeth. If we use the 1958 registration figures (our earliest) to analyze his two previous constituencies, we can see that the potential black vote would have been only 20 percent in his 1946 Georgia house race, and only 17 percent in his 1948 solicitor's race. In a general election like 1966, most of the black constituents who went to the polls doubtless voted for Flynt because he was a Democrat.

Black voters were not relevant elements of his constituency at election time. They knew it and he knew it. In policy matters most dear to them, Jack Flynt did not represent his black constituents. And they were not capable of holding him accountable.

While it was certainly true that Flynt did not have to discuss racial policy when he presented himself at home, it was also true, I concluded, that he did not like to, either. In private he voiced his distaste for politicians who openly played the race card. As if to underscore the point, he drove me to Atlanta to meet and have lunch with former governor Ellis Arnall, a noted Georgia liberal and longtime friend, whom Flynt had supported in an unsuccessful comeback effort against a segregationist in the Democratic primary in 1966.[18]

Even more convincing, however, and more important, was evidence of his preference for deemphasizing any and all policy discussion—at every turn and on every occasion. It was not just that he did not talk to me or to others in my presence about racial policy. He did not talk to me or to others about *any* policy. And that was an essential fact in thinking about his choice of a representational strategy.

Speeches

Had Flynt chosen to articulate or advocate his positions on public policy, he would have done so in his public appearances. In my first two visits, I heard him deliver five speeches, but only one had any overt policy content.

The one exception was a 1970 evening presentation at West Georgia College in Carroll County. Flynt was apprehensive that the audience—not a part of his primary constituency—would be "laying" for him and that he would be walking into a "bear trap." Indeed, he prevailed upon me to delay my departure so that I could provide him with "cover" in the unfamiliar academic setting.

At dinner, however, he warmed to his companions in his best person-to-person style, reaching out to the faculty by wrapping himself in their values. "The greatest compliment you can pay to a faculty member," he said later, "is to say that he stimulates you to think." Flynt let it drop, with self-deprecating humor, that he had been a regional finalist in the 1936 Rhodes scholar competition—and that he had met disaster on a question about Kant's categorical imperative. "I had never heard of it, but I sure found out in a hurry." After a little discussion, he folded the topic neatly into his favorite theme: "One way you can interpret the categorical imperative is to say that each one of us should leave his community a better place than it was when he came into it."

When the discussion moved to the students at the college, he recounted meetings in his Washington office with students from other states on the subject of Vietnam. "I suppose," he said, "that when the New York students saw the 'Georgia' sign outside my office door, they expected to find some redneck." He then went on to emphasize the importance of "opening lines of communication" with students on subjects like the war. And he told the group that his "dialogues" with young people had "recharged my intellectual and spiritual batteries."

Those were the themes Flynt carried into his talk—a brief and very general set of comments on the importance of reducing government spending, controlling the growth of government, and allowing the free market to work. He took the students' pro-government, pro-environment, pro-regulation questions head on, with a minimum of waffling. There were none on civil rights. His conservative views were received, as he said afterward, "without a single discourteous question or action." The heaviest dose of questions concerned Vietnam. The congressman approached them as a means of examining all sides of the question rather than taking a position. His emphasis was on "the free flow of communication," "listening to each side," "disagreeing without being disagreeable." He stated his record of support for the war, while at the same time expressing his reservation about an official policy that did not allow us to win it.

Reflecting on the discussion later, Flynt applied one of his all-purpose, person-to-person prescriptions. "When I disagree with people, I tell them. I don't tell lies to some and the truth to others, so I don't have to remember who I lied to. This helps me with people who don't ordinarily agree with me—school people, labor people, to mention two. I'd rather have a man fall out with me because we disagree on the issue than because he thought I lied to him." Not without a visible sense of relief, he claimed to have "enjoyed it." Driving home, he stopped at two friends' homes to tell them all about the evening ("If they hear a knock on the door after eleven o'clock, they know it's me"). I counted the event a successful personal connection and a policy standoff.

"He's a very nice and very honest man," a liberal history professor from the college said to me afterward. "I like him very much. He's very open to his constituents in helping them. And he has the power to do it. But he's far too conservative for me. I'll vote for him, though, because he's so nice and so powerful. I'll only vote against him if some charismatic liberal comes along." He added that a group of liberals in the district had started organizing to find someone of their persuasion to run against Flynt. Unbeknownst to the professor, however, that "charismatic liberal" would turn out to be his first-year history department colleague, Newt Gingrich.

Flynt's other four speeches in 1970 and 1972 had themes of community attachments and stability. They were delivered to strong supporters and were designed to identify him with his primary constituency at the community level, as he had identified himself with individual supporters in his personal contacts.

In his 1972 sesquicentennial celebration speech in Pike County (population 7,300), for example, he reached for every possible linkage. "I feel as much at home in Pike County as if I had been born here and lived here every day of my life," he declared. "I remember coming to Zebulon [the county seat] with my father more than fifty years ago." "The original deed to the home in which I was born was drawn up in Pike County." "I came to Pike County many times when I was solicitor." And, "My grandfather fought side by side and shoulder to shoulder with Pike County men in the Confederate Army in the War between the States."

Two days later, speaking from the pulpit of a nearby country church celebrating its homecoming, Flynt began, "I have never recognized the artificial boundaries that separate our two counties. I have felt as much at home in this county—our county—among my friends and neighbors for over fifty years as I have in my home county." And he topped off the event by sharing a neighborly, community-cooked "dinner on the grounds."

He began his speech to the Business and Professional Women's Club in Butts County with the remark that "I feel as much at home in Butts County as I do any place on earth." And, recalling the biblical story of Moses taking off his shoes on holy ground, he continued, "I can't begin to describe to you the frustration I feel when I see these crazy experiments in social reform and when I watch them move this country from strength to weakness instead of from strength to greater strength. These frustrations would make me a nervous wreck or worse if I could not come back home to be with you, my friends and neighbors, my supporters and my constituents. I come home to refresh my spirit and renew my strength, here in the heart of west-central Georgia, where my family's roots go deep. To me, this is truly holy ground."

With the exception of the reference to crazy experiments in Washington—which I took to be a code word for civil rights legislation, particularly school busing—the speech contained no specific policy content. Flynt knew, for example, that the Equal Rights Amendment was of great interest to the women's group, and he had discussed his opposition to it with them in private. But he never touched on it in his public talk.

In each speech, the congressman presented himself to his constituents as a member of a common community and invited them to think of him as a representative who is "one of us." His message, both "given and given off,"[19] was "I am like you; I feel at home with you; I identify with you; I understand you; I have walked in your shoes; I can put myself in your shoes; we are part of the same community; I hear your concerns; I will look out for your interests; I will do what you would do if you were in my place. You can trust me." In sum, "I represent you because I identify with you, and because we are so much like each other." That message did not require overt policy pronouncements. It required only Flynt's constant personal contact, personal service, and personal accessibility—and a solid reputation for the same.

At the end of my 1972 visit, I wrote that "the entire four day performance was totally and completely *issueless*. The articulated, visible content of politics is personal and communitarian, not issues. On the one occasion where the meeting concerned an issue (the environment), that was the one occasion when Jack, by choice, said *nothing*. He sat all evening in the Jackson High School auditorium amid much citizen agitation over water pollution, and said *nothing*" (emphasis in original).

My observation that Flynt avoided policy discussion was corroborated by an outside report on an interview session he had had with the Macon League of Women Voters, which read, "In an effort to focus politics on issues, the League of Women Voters chapter members made an hour long appointment with their congressman in 1970. They drew up a list of problems they wished to discuss. Flynt received them cordially in his office in Macon. Showing little interest in the problems the women had come to discuss, he took up most of the hour exploring the case of a Chicago welfare recipient who was said to have stayed in an expensive hotel at the government 'expense.'" After that experience, said one league member, "we finally gave up on Mr. Flynt."[20] They were asking him to do something he was deeply disinclined to do.

Flynt's public speeches revealed more interest in community maintenance than in public policy. His purpose was to talk about the many things that linked him to his white constituents and to present himself as a maintainer of, and spokesman for, their common interests. He was a master of bonds, links, ties, and memories. The idea is that, as William Bianco has argued, the more constituents perceive they have interests in common with the representative, the more they will trust that representative on the issues.[21] For Flynt, the "he is one of us" and "I am one of you" linkages were the underpinning that kept his person-intensive representational strategy viable. However, had he not been in a district with sufficient homogeneity to allow him to assert that "I am one of you," it would not have been as easy for him to adopt the representational strategy he did. Conversely, had his district been more heterogeneous, it would have been harder for him to pursue a dominantly person-intensive strategy.

In speeches, as in personal contact, Flynt deliberately steered clear of anything that might divide representative and constituents or subject their fundamental issue consensus to scrutiny. He concluded all four "I am one of you" speeches with the same peroration: "When the final summons comes, as it must come to us all, when it comes time for us to draw our final breath, and when the last words pass between our mortal lips—audibly or inaudibly—if we can say we have left this a better community, a better country than it was when we found it, if we can say that we have done, each in his own way, something to move our community, our country from strength to greater strength, if we say this, we will not have lived in vain."

His message to his listeners was that they belonged to a community—from past to present to future, from individual to locality to nation—and that he and they together should work to keep it and make it better. In a political sense, the message was calibrated to obviate or depress factionalism in a one-party district. It encapsulated the comfortable, durable, me-in-the-constituency fit that Jack Flynt had negotiated with his primary constituency and beyond.

Votes

In Jack Flynt's speeches about community connections, the conservative policy consensus that underpinned that community was left implicit. But it became very explicit when he acted in Congress. There his social conservatism was invoked in votes that opposed civil rights, gun control, abortion, the Equal Rights Amendment, and restrictions on prayer in the public schools. His economic conservatism was reflected in votes in opposition to Medicare, public housing, and federal aid to education and in support of reductions in spending across the board—except where the military was involved. His support for textiles was seen in his protectionist votes against reciprocal trade and in his lobbying efforts aimed at the executive branch to protect cotton prices. And his support for agriculture was shown in votes upholding price support programs.

For the years 1955–61, Americans for Democratic Action (ADA) gave Flynt the following liberalism scores (ranked from 0 to 100) on votes chosen by them as definitive: 1955, 10; 1956, 0; 1957, 0; 1958, 0; 1959, 0; 1960, 0; 1961, 20. Out of sixty-seven votes that were deemed by the ADA to separate liberals from conservatives in the House in the period 1955–61, Jack Flynt cast only five "liberal" votes. And those extremely conservative years were his formative years in terms of his constituency relationships.

In the context of a conservative policy consensus at home, Flynt believed that he enjoyed considerable leeway in voting. He felt very few constituency constraints. About his voting decisions, he made two generalizations. First, "The votes I cast in Congress satisfy the people in my district—not because I set out to satisfy them, but because we think alike on most issues. They don't disagree with me on anything, not anything they are likely to get mad about." Second, "I have more freedom in voting than almost anyone I know. Many times, I vote in ways that are not popular with my constituents, and I know they aren't popular. They know how I vote, but they will listen to me and let me explain. And they trust me." By his lights, this was true. He did, indeed, enjoy the leeway he had so laboriously negotiated with his constituency. The examples he cited, however, suggested that his leeway existed mostly on matters that did not threaten the consensus or on matters where his information was recognizably superior to that of his constituents.

For example, in support of his assertion that "I have taken unpopular stands and then swung them around to my way of thinking," he cited a vote to uphold President Eisenhower's veto of a public works bill. "Some of my friends," he said, "had some things in it they thought were for them." But he defined the issue as "excessive spending," and "once I explained the budgetary situation to them, there was no problem." Similarly, Flynt asserted that "some members of the Georgia delegation vote against almost all appropriations bills. I vote against some, but I vote for a lot of them. If anyone tries to criticize me on that, I know so much about those bills that I would cut them to ribbons." His expertise as a member of the Appropriations Committee gave him a great deal of latitude in explaining spending decisions to the folks back home.

When I pushed him and asked him point blank if he could cast "liberal" votes, he said, "Yes." He recounted two such votes. First, "I voted with Speaker McCormack in 1963 to keep the Rules Committee at fifteen instead of going back to twelve, whereas I had voted against Sam Rayburn to keep it at twelve. It became an issue in my 1996 campaign. I don't think it cost me one vote." And second, "I marched up on Christmas Eve and voted to send wheat to Russia. That was a bad vote as far as my constituents were concerned, and it was a bad vote logically. It was the biggest issue ever created by one of my votes. My opponent made a lot of that in 1966. But I don't think it cost me one vote." The congressman had achieved his goal of inter-election support and a measure of voting leeway.

Given his view that these two "liberal" votes had become campaign issues, however, I asked him if his 1966 Republican opponent had attacked him as a liberal. "He tried at first to paint me as a liberal," said Flynt, "and, failing that, he tried to out-conservative me. No matter how hard he tried, he couldn't out-conservative me. There just wasn't any room. If he got on the conservative side of me, he'd fall off into the air." Or, as Flynt put it during that campaign, "If anything, I've probably voted more conservatively than the people of this district would have wanted."[22] His first general election contest, like his first primary election contest, pivoted on personal, rather than policy, differences.

In the picture Flynt painted, his policy connections—as of 1970 and 1972—seem not to have placed heavy demands upon him or to have threatened him on grounds that made it hard for him to defend the status quo. None of the voting problems he cited threatened his comfortable position within the philosophical consensus of his primary constituency.

Vietnam

To these generalizations about Congressman Flynt's lack of policy involvements, there was one exception—which only served to confirm the strength of his representational relationships. He decided, after a career as a national defense hawk—a career marked by undeviating support for the American military—that he could no longer support the war in Vietnam. He made the decision, he said, in December 1970, just weeks after his session with the students at West Georgia College.

He cast his first vote for a new policy four months later in a speech opposing the extension of the military draft. He said, in part,

> Never in my life, certainly never since I have been in Congress, have I been confronted with a decision as difficult as my decision to oppose this bill. . . . For many years, the people of the Sixth District of Georgia cried out with almost one voice, "Win the war in Vietnam." Then that one voice was changed to "Win the war in Vietnam or get out." Today the people of the Sixth District have

become convinced that the United States is not going to win the war in Indochina and they have now changed that one voice to say, "Get out of Indochina." The only way I know to get out of Indochina is to stop the drafting of young Americans to fight there.[23]

It was one vote of his career that attracted national attention, precisely because it came from a pro-military, conservative congressman from a part of the country most strongly predisposed to support any national military effort. The morning after, a front-page story in the *New York Times* called it "a break in the once solid Southern flank" of support.[24]

Flynt, however, cast it as a decision totally in agreement with his constituency. And by every indication, it was. But it was a policy decision of a magnitude that required that he explain it to his constituents. He did this in the period between his private decision and his vote in the House, arguing that we should get out of Vietnam because, given the limitations we had imposed upon ourselves in fighting the war, it was unwinnable.

"I'll tell you a position of mine that did *not* bring in critical mail," he exclaimed in 1972. "My speech against the war. I was very apprehensive about the effect it would have in the district. I didn't really know how people felt, and I was being pessimistic. But it was something I had to do. As it turned out, only a very few wrote in criticizing me, and many, many wrote favorable letters. The one-on-one response was totally favorable. It turned out that their thinking was just about the same as mine on the subject." Given Flynt's propensity to avoid policy talk, the decision was a risk. But given his solid, "one of us" relationship with his constituents, it was not.

Moreover, he had taken some preparatory soundings with the group of constituents most likely to disagree with him, the American Legion. "The rank and file of the American Legion have been 100 percent supporters of Jack Flynt," he said. "I thought they would get mad at me for publicly breaking with the president's policy over Vietnam. But I haven't lost a single one. Actually, I tried my position on for size before an American Legion group [in Griffin] prior to the time I made my speech on the floor of the House. It turned out that I was saying what they were thinking, but [they] didn't know how to say it." It was a case in which the congressman became a policy leader in his district not by changing constituents' minds, but by giving voice to a latent view of theirs that was waiting to be formulated and expressed. In the end, it only confirmed how closely in touch with district sentiment their "one of us" congressman really was.

As Flynt saw it, moreover, he persuaded other members of the Georgia delegation to turn against the war. He also served as a liaison between the liberal opponents of the war and his group of pro-military opponents of the war. "I played a part, and perhaps a major part," he said, "in ending the war in Southeast Asia. If I had been fighting for my political life back home, I could not have played the part—the major part—I did. I used every chip I had and called in every IOU I had to get support for what I accomplished in ending the Vietnam War."[25] However accurate this self-portrait may be, Flynt's policy involvement on Vietnam was the most entrepreneurial and the most visible of his political career.

The constituents on whom Jack Flynt depended for their inter-election support and to whom he gave so much personal attention were not a high-demand constituency, at least not in terms of their visible demands. He told a reporter during his Vietnam efforts that the most letters he had ever received criticizing a vote of his was six.[26] It was not a district bulging with aggressive, new-style policy ad-vocacy groups. Even where their most deeply held policy prefer-ences were involved, constituents did not call upon or expect their representative to launch high-profile activity. Flynt's media appear-ances could be—and were, as we shall see in Chapter 3—few and far between. His constituents seemed content to have him pursue his own preferences for person-to-person engagement. And that attitude helps explain his success in doing so.

Party Connections

While each House member is pursuing an electoral career in the district, he or she is simultaneously pursuing an institutional career in the House.[27] That career is driven by the pursuit of influence—as committee member, as party decision maker, as factional leader, as debater, and as voter on the House floor. The simultaneous pursuit of the two careers necessarily connects one to the other. And the crucial connecting link is the political party.

Both the institutional career of the member and the monitoring judgments of his or her constituents begin with their connection to the party. For the representative, it is the party that organizes the House and superintends the distribution of positions and resources inside the House. For the constituents, the party label is their most elementary connection to their representative.[28] Indeed, the representational process begins when an aspiring politician captures the party label. Once elected, the politician carries that label into the House and pursues the goal of inside influence largely within the boundaries set by his or her congressional party organization.

In the District: The Party Label

Jack Flynt captured the party label in the Democratic primary of 1954, and his person-intensive activities ever since then were directed at keeping it. In a one-party district, the strong support of a primary constituency was all he needed to be elected to Congress. Those supporters were the people with whom he spent most of his time during my visits. He was not the product of a party organization. He dismissed the locally organized parties as merely "technical entities, mostly poll pullers." Were he ever to face a general election, the party label would also connect him to a much broader reelection constituency. For these voters, too, the party label would be their main connection to a candidate. For them, "Democrat" would be an acceptable definition of "a good representative."

Flynt's "travel talk" often touched on his proprietary, "king of the hill" attitude toward the Democratic Party label and his determination to keep it. He was acutely aware of the ways in which incumbent strength gets tested and measured by watchful constituents. He wanted to convey the kind of strength—personal and political—that would persuade other Democrats not to challenge him. His accounts of past activities became an inventory of his political invulnerability. First was his proven electoral strength:

[In 1946] there were four people running for two [Georgia] house seats. Out of 7,000 votes, I got 6,400. The next man got 3,300, and the next man was ten behind him. In the 1954 primary, I intended to win. I worked like hell, campaigned hard and effectively. I lost Clayton to the man who lived there, and Meriwether and Troup by a little bit. I carried twelve of the fifteen counties. And neither of my [two] opponents ran consistently first or second. [Flynt spent $27,000 to do this, $23,000 of which was his own money.]

In 1966 I ran against the most popular Republican in the state of Georgia. He had been elected twice to the state legislature from Bibb County, and he was Republican state chairman. A friend told me his strategy. He was sure he would come out of Bibb County with a 15,000-vote majority and also carry Spalding, my home county. Then he said he didn't care what happened in the other thirteen counties. . . . I carried all fifteen. I carried Spalding, and I beat him by 3,000 votes in Bibb County. . . . He had never lost an election, and everyone thought he was invulnerable. I beat him in Bibb County by about 55 percent to 45 percent. But [even] if I had gotten 50.000 [percent], it would have been a smashing victory. We took a Republican county and made it Democratic. [And] in the county [Troup] where the Republican candidate for governor was born, I pulled a bigger vote than he did. I ran ahead of the party. [Flynt spent $75,000 in this campaign.]

Second was his ability to head off a potential challenge: "The only division in my [original] district was between the east side and the west side of the Flint River. I never faced that conflict, because I was determined to go into the west side of the river in force. By that I mean I worked from the beginning to establish myself there. The result was that they never did run anyone against me from the west side of the Flint."

Third, Flynt touted his ability to thwart outside predators: "They tried to gut me [in the 1966 redistricting]. . . . I woke up one morning and found that the legislature had given me a district that reached all the way to Columbus, included Macon, and left me with only three of the fifteen counties I had. I managed to fix that up in a hurry. Eventually I lost two small counties and picked up two medium-sized counties and one large county [Bibb]."

To this strength he added a readiness to take tough retaliatory action against personally motivated attacks. Speaking of a once-powerful sheriff he had sent to jail, Flynt declared: "He sent a message to me that if ever he saw me on the street or if I ever came within his line of vision, he was going to, and I quote, 'stomp hell out of me.' I sent back a message that I was ready, and that if that day ever came, he had better kill me because if he didn't, I would kill him, so help me God. He also told a group of supporters that he would put up $75,000 for anyone who would run against me. . . . I was just waiting for someone to run against me so that I could wrap that threat around his neck."

A final testimony to Flynt's power was his performance in Washington: "Nothing is more damaging to a congressman in his district than to have his constituents believe that he doesn't have the power to get something he wants. . . . See that [Coweta County] Federal Building and United States Courthouse? I worked my head off to get that building. The people here were fixing to run someone against me if I hadn't produced it."

All of these strengths were underscored by his competitiveness. Flynt had no intention of losing: "[When the time comes] I'll announce my retirement myself. I am not going to be pushed out by anybody. I want to go out in my own way and at a time of my own choosing." When I once asked him how an opponent might knock him off his perch, he said, "It's such a negative thing. I can't conceive of it."

Jack Flynt was king of the hill. He owned the party label, and he intended to keep it. I watched as he made himself personally accessible to the people who helped him do that.

In the House: The Party Organization

The individual member's search for power inside the House of Representatives depends on the organization of power there. And it is the congressional parties that organize the House—by selecting its leaders, controlling its committees, and prescribing its procedure.[29] Jack Flynt entered the House at a time when it was controlled and organized by the Democratic majority. The party's majority, however, was divided into two increasingly divided ideological wings—a larger wing of liberal northerners and a smaller wing of conservative southerners. As a conservative southern Democrat, Flynt often had to choose between loyalty to his party organization in the House and loyalty to his strongest party supporters in the constituency.

From 1955 to 1962, Jack Flynt pursued his institutional career in Sam Rayburn's House. And Speaker Rayburn, as Joseph Cooper and David Brady have demonstrated, was dependent on an ad hoc, informal, personal bargaining style to secure Democratic majorities. "[He] had to mobilize a majority party fairly evenly balanced between discordant northern and southern elements, confronted a set of committees and committee chairmen with great power and autonomy and had to deal with individual members who rejected party discipline and prized their independence."[30] Flynt's aspirations for influence inside the House had to be processed through Sam Rayburn, and they were subject to the kind of personal bargaining that Rayburn relied on to lead his party.

On a passive/aggressive scale of inside power-seeking, Flynt was mostly passive. He was content to let his career in the House develop through the patronage of others and the accumulation of seniority on his committee. When he was a freshman, the Georgia delegation secured for him an assignment to a good committee, Interstate and Foreign Commerce—Sam Rayburn's old committee. But Flynt did not go out of his way, as a member of that committee, to ingratiate himself with the Speaker. In his recollections, he was anxious to highlight their differences. Two examples come to mind.

Early in his House career, Flynt had cast a vote in the committee against a bill exempting natural gas from federal regulation, and his side had won. The Speaker asked him for procedural help—of a sort that fellow partisans are normally expected to render to their leaders.

When I got back to my office, my secretary told me that the Speaker's office was on the line. I said, "Tell them to wait a minute." She said, "Well, it's the Speaker himself on the line." So I picked it up, and Mr. Rayburn said, "We have chosen you to make the motion to reconsider today's natural gas vote when the committee meets again in the morning." I said, "I voted against the measure." He said, "I know that. But, as you know, a motion to reconsider must be made by a person who was on the prevailing side of the original vote. You don't have to vote for the motion. We have the votes. All you have to do is make the motion to reconsider."

I said, "Mr. Speaker, I can't do that. I've already made up my mind. And I want the bill defeated." He said, "Why don't you think about it tonight and we'll get back to you in the morning." I said, "It won't make any difference. My answer will be the same tomorrow as it is now, and it will be same next week as it is tomorrow." Mr. Rayburn listened and said, "Son, I've been in the House for over forty years, and let me tell you one thing. Those who go along most, get along best."

A couple of years later, Flynt voted to support President Eisenhower's veto of the public works appropriation. "I cast my vote and left the House floor. [Georgia colleague] Prince Preston called me and asked me to come back." Preston, Majority Leader John McCormack, and Speaker Rayburn tried to get him to change his vote. "I was the deciding vote. Sam Rayburn shook his finger in my face and said to me, 'The people of your district will never forgive you for this.' I said, 'Mr. Rayburn, I can vote conservative or I can vote liberal, and my constituents don't care. But if I vote one way at two o'clock and another way at two-thirty, they'll think they sent an idiot to Congress. I can't do it.' Sam Rayburn never forgave me for that."

In both of these cases, Flynt placed his highest priority on taking a policy position and sticking to it, as if that stubborn independence was a reputation his constituents would expect and value, particularly if they saw him standing against the pressure of the more liberal national party. Further, because he never had to commit himself strongly before the home folks, he had an additional increment of flexibility in the institutional context.

When forced to make a choice, Jack Flynt was more protective of his constituency career at home than he was of his institutional career in the House. And more often than most Democrats, he was forced to make that choice.

In January 1961 Speaker Rayburn put Flynt's policy views in direct conflict with the furtherance of his institutional career. The Speaker had put his own power and prerogatives on the line, more publicly than ever, by supporting the enlargement ("packing") of the conservative-dominated Rules Committee. The committee, with power to control floor action, had become an obstacle to the passage of liberal legislation; the stakes for the program of newly elected President John Kennedy were great. The vote gathering process was intense, and the prospects were in doubt. Coincidentally, the Georgia delegation was making a bid to fill a vacancy on the powerful House Appropriations Committee. The Democratic leadership offered it to Flynt, *if* he would agree to vote with the Speaker in favor of the Rules Committee enlargement. Flynt's policy views were completely in tune, however, with those of the existing conservative majority of the Rules Committee, and he was strongly opposed to any change. He assumed his supportive constituency at home would be opposed as well.

As Flynt told the story,

I didn't especially want to go on [the Appropriations Committee]. But the delegation wanted me to. It's very important to a state like Georgia to have a man on the committee, and we can't get on the committee in our first term—maybe Illinois, but not Georgia. The people senior to me had positions, so I was it. Well, we got embroiled in the Rules Committee fight. I had it put to me directly: "If you want to go on the Appropriations Committee, you should vote for the enlargement of the Rules Committee." I said, "I don't want it that bad." And I might have said, "I don't give a damn whether I get on or not." I was happy on Interstate and Foreign Commerce. That's a good committee and I [would have] had to give up my seniority there.

He unhesitatingly chose to forgo the pursuit of inside power in order to vote his policy preferences and those of his constituents. Indeed, so strongly did he feel about his choice that he expressed a withering contempt for at least one Georgia colleague who "sold out" on that vote in order to keep his inside influence. Needless to say, Flynt did not get the committee assignment.

But that was not the end of the story. Constituents do have expectations, usually latent, about the power of their representative. Some of Jack Flynt's constituents, particularly some newspapers, interpreted the loss of the Appropriations slot as evidence that their representative was powerless to get what he wanted inside the House. At that suggestion, Flynt's king-of-the-hill impulses took over. Such a constituency opinion, he said, "might have been the *only* issue in the campaign in 1962. I didn't want to get beat over the head with that by someone who didn't know what he was talking about. And no one in the world would have believed me unless I went out and did it." "Nothing," he elaborated later, "is more damaging to a congressman in his district than to have his constituents believe that he doesn't have the power to get something he wants of that nature. That would have been all that was needed—and *only* that—to defeat me in my district. So, once that story was printed, I had to try for Appropriations again, and I had to win. So I set about to do it. When a vacancy opened up a year later, I had [the votes of] thirteen out of the fifteen members of the Committee on Committees." This time Flynt was successful. "By that time," he added, "Mr. Rayburn had died. I'm not sure I could have made it if Mr. Rayburn was still there."

Flynt's preference was to let his institutional career take its own course. But he had been forced into actively pursuing the goal of inside power because he believed that constituency opinion might be turned against him if he did not. In time, therefore, the visible exercise of influence inside the institution entered his mix of goals. As his seniority increased on the Appropriations Committee, he invoked that position in touting his responsiveness to his constituency at home. A sequence of career-related events had led him to adjust his goals and his representational strategy.

His relationship with the Democratic Party leadership in the House was one of constant tension. He was a dyed-in-the-wool Democrat, by birth and by career. His father had been, for four years, chairman of the state Democratic Executive Committee. For many years Jack Flynt Jr. was a party whip for his region. And near the end of his career, the Democratic leadership chose him for the delicate job of chairman of the House Committee on Standards and Official Conduct, that is, the Ethics Committee—if not a sign of party affection, at least a sign of party respect. There was not a Republican bone in his body. But there were Republican-like policies in his head.

On the House floor, Flynt often left his party's majority to vote in favor of the most conservative fiscal policy. In the twenty years from 1956 to 1976, he voted with the majority of his fellow Democrats an average of 31 percent of the time. The average party unity score for all House Democrats during that period was twice as high, at 64 percent. When a majority of southern Democrats voted with a majority of Republicans to form "the conservative coalition," Flynt joined the group more often than not—more often even than most other southern Democrats. His average pro–conservative coalition score, from 1959 to 1978, was a high 74 percent agreement, compared to an average score of 59 percent agreement for all southern Democrats.[31] Inside the Appropriations Committee, he was happily ensconced among a bipartisan group of budget cutters.[32] By 1964 he was, in his words, "on the two most important subcommittees, Defense and State, Justice, Commerce, and Judiciary."

Back home, Flynt found pragmatic solutions to the conflict between party label and policy independence. On the side of party loyalty, he campaigned actively for John Kennedy in 1960. And he recalled, with pride, that he had given support to Democrat Lyndon Johnson in 1964, despite LBJ's unpopularity in his district. The textile industry had been anxious to change price regulations on cotton, he recalled. "We asked Ike. He didn't know what we were talking about. He turned it over to his secretary of commerce, and nothing was ever done. We asked Jack Kennedy. He promised us some help but never did anything about it. But LBJ pitched in and helped us get one-price cotton. After his help, I felt I owed him something. So not only did I support him in 1964, but I went down to meet him in Miami and rode with him to Macon and sat beside him on the platform. I never heard so many boos from an audience, but I sat right up there with him. I felt I owed it to him after what he did for us." Flynt campaigned on his work for one-price cotton. And Barry Goldwater carried the district.[33]

In 1968, however, Flynt finessed his party loyalty. With locally popular George Wallace on the presidential ballot, the congressman offered no support to his party's standard-bearer and civil rights symbol, Hubert Humphrey. "I didn't say one single thing about the national race. Not one single word did I utter. I stayed out entirely and completely. I told a few close friends how I was going to vote, but to my knowledge, none of them ever said a word. At least, it never came back to haunt me." In the 1976 presidential election, he had no choice but to support his popular fellow Georgian, Jimmy Carter—despite their sharp differences on policy.

CHAPTER THREE

Jack Flynt, 1972–1976

Change and Challenge

Contextual Change

Between 1960 and 1970, the population of Georgia became increasingly less rural and more suburban. Jack Flynt's transitional district (1966–70) occupied a pivotal location in the path of that shift. The burgeoning Atlanta metropolitan area was exploding into the near suburbs and gradually pushing southward toward the small rural counties that formed the core of Flynt's political support. By 1970 the Sixth District's population far exceeded the statewide average (by 17 percent), and it had to be brought into equality with the other districts. Boundary changes were inevitable. Nonetheless, said Flynt, "no district in Georgia was changed as much as mine was." And the change was legislated against his wishes. "Clearly," he said, it was "an effort to defeat me."

His preferences had been made clear to all. Flynt wanted to give up his fastest-growing county, suburban Clayton County, in exchange for two or three equivalent small counties farther from Atlanta. He wanted, that is, to shift his population base southward, away from the metropolitan area. He wanted to keep the small city of Macon in Bibb County and to add some nearby counties, thus maintaining his long-standing representational patterns and his solid representational fit.

But that is exactly what did *not* happen. Instead, Bibb County and five other small, familiar counties nearby were taken away from him. His district was pushed northward into the near suburbs of Atlanta and up to the city line (see map 3). He picked up 120,000 unwanted and unfamiliar suburbanites on the southern rim of At-

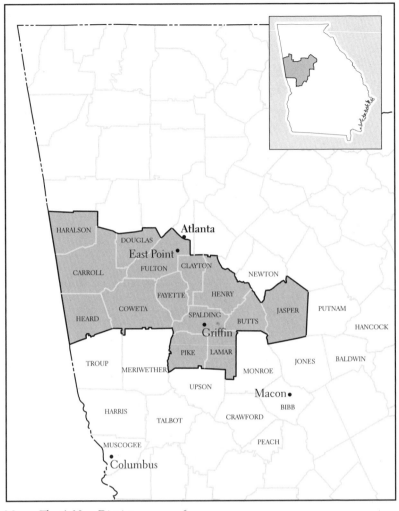

Map 3. Flynt's New District, 1972–1976
(Georgia's Sixth Congressional District)

lanta's own Fulton County, along with 30,000 more in suburban
Douglas County. Taken together, Clayton, South Fulton, and Douglas made up 54 percent of the population in his new district.

These suburbanites presented a different demographic profile and
a different "active electorate" than the one that had dominated in
Flynt's two earlier districts. In his "one of us" formula, the "us" was
changing. His new constituents were the products of southern economic development—younger, better educated, and more mobile.
They were middle-class entrepreneurs. They were good-government
reformers who attacked courthouse elites and advocated two-party

competition. Some were widely connected businessmen—"in banks and insurance companies," he said. There were 7 percent fewer black Democrats, but the civil rights movement had brought more organization and activism among these black constituents. And the district now had a larger number of organized, active, white Republicans, who brought different economic interests. An estimated 6,000 of them worked for Delta Airlines, for example. "My public reaction," the congressman said, "was that I always liked every district I ever had, that I knew I would like every district I ever would have, that I hoped the new people in my district would like me as much as I liked them. Privately, I said, 'It's an abomination.'" Redistricting threatened the representational equilibrium he had negotiated and protected for seventeen years.

The redistricting propelled Flynt into a context in which his established representational strategy would be challenged, too, by the prospect of increased policy conflict between his old and new constituencies. The first specific conflict I observed in 1972 involved the environment. And the first clue came when I spotted a "Save the Flint" bumper sticker. (Only two years earlier, I had stood overlooking the Flint River, listening to the congressman and three Upson County officials exulting over the prospect of the very project—the Sprewell Bluff Dam—that the bumper sticker now assailed.) The next day I accompanied him to a meeting of the Coalition for Pollution Control, at which we were handed a pamphlet urging people to "Save the Flint," and at which we heard an official of the Georgia League of Conservation Voters urging people to lobby their public officials on the matter.

Issue conflict had arisen between the suburban and rural sections of the district, whereas in his previous districts, there had been no conflict. Like many pro-business legislators, Flynt was uncomfortable with environmental issues, and he said nothing at the meeting.[1] Whatever his ultimate stand might be, it would be costly. This was one more difficulty the longtime incumbent did not need or want— and one that he was not well prepared for.

The question arose as to how, or whether, he would adapt his established person-intensive, personal accessibility strategy to his new circumstances. A major incentive for rethinking the matter was the prospect of renewed electoral competition. As Flynt interpreted the context, 1972 was no problem, but 1974 would be another matter. "In the short run, it's just perfect. No one will run against me from the old part of the district because they will figure I have the old part locked solid. And no one from the new part will run against me because they will figure the incumbent has an advantage in any area where neither is known. But that will last for only two years. I'll never be able to keep everyone in that district happy." Given this reading of the situation, the question was whether he would remain in a protectionist mode and work to maintain his long-run goal of interelection support, or whether he would revert to an expansionist outlook and devote himself more single-mindedly to the immediate goal of reelection.

Jack Flynt was not unfamiliar with suburbia. He had represented a suburban county—Clayton—since 1954. But Clayton was the one county that he had never understood and had never cultivated successfully. He had not carried it in the 1954 primary. It had always been the odd one out, the county in which he had never been at home, the one in which he had the least sense that he was "one of us." "I should write a book about this district—beginning with the Indians," he told me. "Nobody knows it like I do. It's a very historic district and a very cohesive district—*except* for Clayton County." Clayton was the only county he had explicitly asked to have taken away from him in the redistricting. But not only had the redistricting left him with Clayton, it had also given him 150,000 new constituents who looked very much like those in Clayton.

Flynt perceived Clayton County and its suburban-style politics as "heterogeneous, disorganized, and full of factions. . . . It doubled in population between 1950 and 1960, and it doubled again between 1960 and 1970. It's bitterly divided . . . split right down the middle on everything. You can't know what they want." "So," I asked, "how do you deal with the county?" "Very cautiously," he replied. For eighteen years, his strategy had been to leave it alone. "Some of my good friends in Clayton criticize me and say I neglect it unduly. And they have a point. But I can get nearly 50 percent of the vote in Clayton County without campaigning there at all. And I couldn't get more than 55 percent if I campaigned there *all* the time. And if I did that, I would become identified with one of the factions and half the people would hate me. And on top of that, I would lose a lot of support elsewhere in the district. It's not worth it."

He had left Clayton County and his interests there in the hands of others, two of its longtime Democratic officeholders and "lifelong friends." "They are the two stabilizing forces in Clayton County. They have been in office—either in the state senate or on the county commission—ever since I have been in Clayton County politics. They have my interests at heart, and I rely very heavily on them to tell me what I have to do to keep from drowning." In a constantly changing context, this absentee strategy seemed like a risky substitute for his personal presence. In any case, it was a very different representational strategy than the one he had employed successfully and for so long in the rest of the district.

During most of his tenure, Clayton County could be ignored politically. In 1954 its population of 23,000 had made up only 8 percent of Flynt's constituency. By 1972, however, the county had grown to 98,000 people. It represented 22 percent of his new constituency, and it could no longer be ignored. It had become politically important in its own right. And it had become important, too, as the leading indicator of Flynt's strategy in adapting to the suburban part of his district. His absentee representational strategy for Clayton and his inadequate working knowledge of the suburban constituency there did not augur well for his cultivation of the large chunk of suburban territory he was now representing.

Suburban Clayton County posed a negotiating problem for Flynt because it did not have the recognizable, approachable communities that characterized his rural counties and the well-bounded city of Macon. He was used to representing stable communities with recognizable economic and political elites, with familiar social structures, with established lines of communication, and with small, homogeneous, white electorates. These were the kinds of communities he had grown up with, could relate to, and felt at home with—communities in which he and his constituents could feel that he was "one of us." They were communities with which he shared basic policy interests and basic expectations about good representation. On that basis, he could negotiate a representational equilibrium in which he gave constituents personal accessibility, they gave him trust and leeway, and neither had an incentive to change the balance.

Strategic Challenge

Flynt's benign neglect of Clayton County registered during our September 1972 tour of his new district. We spent several hours driving around "exploring" the South Fulton County area. It was the first time I had ever seen the congressman without any idea of where to go or what to do. In the recent primary, he had crushed a weak opponent from the area. And for quite a while, we drove up and down the street on which he thought the opponent lived, to see if we could identify his home by "a Cadillac and a boat" in the driveway. It was one of the least purposeful adventures imaginable. He was simply baffled. At one point he exclaimed, "Well, we've been exploring the new district for an hour and we haven't seen one person yet." Not, that is, any that he knew or that knew him. We had, of course, seen many hundreds of people, but he had not connected personally with a single one of them—as he surely would have done, over and over again, in the old parts of the district. For someone whose basic idea of representation featured personal contact, the place was bewildering. Uncertainty had been introduced into a relationship where certainty had once prevailed.

"How would you campaign in this district?" he wondered out loud as we rode along.

> It's going to have to be an entirely different kind of campaign for me. People are going to be hard to reach. You can't do it by TV because you reach less than 15 percent of the market you pay for. Economics rules that out. And there's no focal point of interest, no incorporated, cohesive areas. It will have to be done on an individual basis. In the primary, the substantial, intelligent people—the businessmen, community leaders, educators, the people I like to have on my side, and I don't mean to neglect the rank and file— these people took me completely on faith. It wasn't that they knew me. They just didn't want the clown who was running against me.

His task would be to find, and to negotiate for the support of, "the substantial people" in the area—achieving the kind of "elite certification" he had won earlier in his settled counties. But the lack of easily identifiable, relatively stable community structures would make it difficult for him.

What is worse, Flynt did not seem open to the adoption of campaign practices appropriate to the suburbs. As we circled the storefronts in the huge Greenbrier shopping mall, he commented, "To my way of thinking, campaigning in shopping centers is a complete and total waste of time. I may be wrong, but I believe that when people are shopping, they don't want to be interrupted by someone handing out political literature." He thus ruled out one of the proven mainstays of most suburban campaigns. In the primary, he said, his friends had urged him to distribute a brochure in the new territory, but he had decided to do no advertising of any sort there. I asked him, "How did you think they would know who you were?" He answered, "I thought they knew me; and if they didn't, I didn't want their support anyway." Coming from a politician who had built a career by forging personal relationships, it seemed to me an inappropriate, if not disoriented, response.

As we started for home, we chanced upon an old country church left standing amid the suburban sprawl, Owl Rock Methodist Church in the Fulton County town of Ben Hill. There, for the first time in our exploration, Flynt connected—with a church and the headstones in the adjoining graveyard. He saw family names he recognized. He jumped out and roamed about enthusiastically, collecting and sorting, as usual, bits of local information: "This church broke off from the Mt. Gilead Baptist Church in 1852." "I never knew Hamilton and his family were buried right here in Fulton County." "I wonder if Mary was any kin of Sarah and John? The dates are about right. Sarah and John moved to College Park in 1921." For twenty minutes, he made person-to-person contacts there in the graveyard just as he did in the old part of the district. But it was troublesome, as well as poignant, that these people could not help him negotiate for support in the new part of the district.

He was encouraged, however, by his initial foray into East Point, the largest city in his new district, for a breakfast talk to the Civitan Club. East Point, like the rest of the new suburban area, had been represented for six years by a very conservative Republican, a man with a career-long ADA liberalism average of zero who had distinguished himself by his vigorous opposition to school busing.[2] As we drove to breakfast, Flynt expressed the confident expectation that his fiscal and social conservatism would give him as supportive a constituency base in the new district as he had had in the old.

He introduced himself to these new constituents as "a neighbor." "We'll get to know each other," he said. "In fact, I feel at home already." He had described them to me as "middle class conservatives," and he presented himself to them as a "fiscal conservative." He decried excessive deficits; he identified himself with "the free enterprise system," and he opined that people should not get "something for nothing." He spoke vaguely about how he would represent them. "When I vote I ask myself first, 'What would a composite of the 460,000 people in the Sixth District do if they had the information I have?' And second, 'What is right for the country regardless of popularity?'" He talked a little about the importance of his role on the Appropriations Committee and ended with his 1972 "final summons" peroration. When he finished, a visitor from the old part of the district jumped up and praised him effusively.

Afterward, the congressman was pleased. "I felt right at home in that group." "Why?" I asked him. "I don't know," he replied. "I can't tell you why; I just did. For one thing, the two men on either side, Ralph Presley and Guy Hill, one's a Delta pilot and the other owns an aircraft maintenance plant. I always feel comfortable when I'm with pilots, military or civilian. King McElwaney, who used to live in Fayetteville, was my constituent there, so he made me feel at home. [Mayor] Bob Brown made it a special point to come to the meeting. And that made me feel at home. His son, Bobby, was there, too. So I guess I have given you some reasons, haven't I?" Typically, all his reasons involved personal connections, not policy connections. I concluded that he had decided to colonize the new part of the district with the identical person-intensive representational strategy that had been so successful for so long in the old part of the district. As he told a friend after the East Point visit, "It went well. I'm going into the new area very slowly, and not by blitz."

At the end of my four-day 1972 visit, when I asked Flynt which of the three speaking events had been the most politically important to him, he demurred. His wife broke in and said, "East Point," because "it was in a new area" and "they were solid people." That was the answer I had expected, but Jack disagreed. "Numbers would have to count for a lot," he said. "So I guess the Pike County sesquicentennial would be first. My whole weekend was built around that because I accepted it at least three months ago. When Marvin [Reid] introduced me there and said there weren't five people out there [out of more than 1,000] who didn't know me, he was probably right. And those who don't know me think they do. . . . Everybody in the community worked to make it a success. That's the kind of thing I want to be part of."

With that assessment came another rule of personal relationships. "If I had said I couldn't make it, they would have understood. They know that if I say I can't come, it's because I honestly can't. But if I had accepted and not shown up, they would have been hurt, and they would never have forgotten it as long as they and I lived. And they would never have forgiven me either. If I hadn't come today, they would have assumed I died."

In second place, Flynt put his talk to the professional women's group in Butts County, as recounted in Chapter 2. By default, the East Point speech was last. This was an indicator that his goal was still durable interelection support and that, therefore, his protectionist-related activities were still the most important to him. He had not embraced an expansionist outlook or expansionist goals. The politician with whom I traveled in 1972 was essentially the same protectionist, path-dependent politician I would have traveled with ten years earlier.

Interim: 1973–1974

As he had predicted, Jack Flynt was reelected in 1972. He was without opposition—for the third straight time—so there was no evidence to be gleaned concerning the efficacy of his strategy. A small indication of his post-1972 reelection efforts in the district can be gleaned, however, by examining his scheduling books for the first seventeen months of his new term, from January 1973 through May 1974. These books show that he made twenty-two trips from Washington to the district for a total of 141 days in the district, including six trips for a total of eighty days during scheduled recesses. The books list seventy separate engagements, for an average of four events per trip. In light of his own maxim that "You can get a lot more votes campaigning in the off years than you can in election years," it was a leisurely reelection campaign schedule.

Arrayed according to the type of group he met with, the engagements included twenty-one talks to civic and/or business groups (Rotary, Kiwanis, Moose, Chamber of Commerce, Jaycees), fourteen talks at schools (high school and college), ten local dedication ceremonies (libraries, hospitals, laboratories), and twenty-five other appearances before various constituent groups (see table 1). Flynt's connections to Main Street business and civic groups remained strong. These were supplemented by his visits to the children of the district. "I try to visit every high school in the district at least [once] every six years. You can reach nearly every generation that way. I find that if I get down off the platform and talk with them, not at them, young people will respond. They don't want to be lectured at. They want me to listen to them. They want to talk things over face to face."

Arrayed by the county in which he appeared, the seventy engagements included seventeen in Fulton County, nine in Clayton

Table 1. Flynt District Engagements, January 1973–May 1974

Type of Engagement	Number
Talks to civic or business groups (Kiwanis, Rotary, Chamber of Commerce, etc.)	21
Talks at high schools and colleges	14
Participation in dedication ceremonies	10
Talks to miscellaneous groups (hospitals, churches, nursing homes)	9
Appearances at parades and party conferences	7
Media appearances (all radio)	4
Undetermined	5
Total	70

Location of Engagement (by County)	Number
Fulton	17
Clayton	9
Spalding	9
Coweta	6
Troup	5
Bibb	3
Heard	2
Henry	2
Eight other counties (1 each)	8
Undetermined	9
Total	70

County, and nine in Spalding County, with the rest scattered among the other counties of the district. Although South Fulton and Clayton did draw more attention than most counties, suburbia (those two plus Douglas) still got proportionately less attention than the rest of the district—37 percent of the appearances for 54 percent of the population. Of thirty-five talks to civic groups, business groups, and school groups—the "substantial people" Flynt wanted most to win over—only ten were in suburbia, not exactly evidence of a strenuous colonizing effort. In sum, the pattern of his appearances leading up the 1974 election presents a picture of a politician who was more protectionist-oriented than expansionist-oriented. He was attending to suburbia, but very definitely "slowly and not by blitz."

In May 1974 I went to Washington to talk with the congressman about his adjustment to the multiple challenges of the new district. He had had twenty months since my September 1972 visit to interpret and to cope with the new demographics, the new community structures, and the new issue conflicts. But he remained uncomfortable and unhappy with their implications for his representational relationships. As he explained, "[In 1970] I represented a district in which my constituents and I had total mutual confidence, respect, and trust—95 percent, nearly 100 percent. Today I have a substantially new district. And 15 to 20 percent of them feel hostility to me because I am new to them. There is a tremendous difference in my ability to represent—and in the pleasure I have in representing—the two districts. The district has changed that much."

Two negotiating worries dominated our conversation. One centered on the new stage of his institutional career; the other centered on his new constituents. A satisfactory representational relationship required, for Flynt, that representative and constituents know each other as part of the same large community—or at least feel that they do. Negotiating such a relationship in the way he always had, however, took a lot of personal contact time in the constituency. And time, he said, had become a problem for him. "I knew nearly everybody in every county in my [original] district—because I had the time to do it or because I made the time to do it. Today, I don't have the time. It's not as easy as it used to be." "I could get 55 percent to 70 percent in these new counties—and South Fulton, too—if I had the time," he added. "I went to Macon in 1966 and ran against the strongest man they had and—with a lot of Macon help—beat him. But I did it in 1966 by neglecting my congressional duties." This time, he said, "I am not going to neglect my duties."

In 1966 Flynt had spent only two terms on the Appropriations Committee, and he had willingly missed 59 percent of the roll-call votes in the House that year. By 1974, however, he had begun to achieve some seniority and some influence on his committee, and he believed that his committee work would—and should—take much more of his time. He saw himself at a different career stage, and he had adopted a new mix of goals.

The decision to put more effort into his institutional career may have been reinforced by the realization that his committee position could be of considerable strategic help to him in cultivating suburbia. When I asked him whether he had any strong supporters in the new area, he said he did. His answer suggested an altered representational strategy, one combining personal contact and institutional influence. "They are people who have known me, or known of me, prior to the time I was placed in their district, [and] also people with whom I have been able to spend as much as four hours, even though they hadn't known me. If I can talk to an intelligent person, I can explain what Congress is all about and my position in the Congress, including my number two position in the Georgia delegation and my tremendous subcommittees on what many people consider the most important committee in Congress. Any professional—educator or businessman—with whom I can talk and explain these things will, in turn, become one of my strongest supporters." The hope implied here was that he now had a selling point he had not had when, through personal effort, he "whipped" the 1966 redistricting in Macon. His increased institutional influence might now be used to compensate for the lack of time in which to win over a new set of constituents.

The more the congressman dealt with these new constituents, however, the more they presented another dilemma. They were a lot less receptive to him than he had expected. The problem was that they were active, committed Republicans. Indeed, most of them had been represented for three terms by a conservative Republican. Still, their resistance to Flynt's overtures puzzled him. Comparing his new district with his two previous ones, he said, "The newness I don't mind; the difference I don't mind. But I run into the situation where individuals and groups whose philosophies coincide with mine are actively against me because they belong to one political party and I belong to another. People, it seems, don't vote philosophy, they vote party. I've never had to contend with that before."

Party had ceased to be a constant in his calculations. It had become a variable. A lot of former Democrats—particularly racial conservatives—were less attached to their party than Jack Flynt was. They, along with newcomers moving from out of state or from the city to the suburbs, were feeding the ranks of the Republican Party. Republicanism in Georgia had become institutionalized, and its new adherents were less susceptible to cross-party voting than before.

For Flynt, that was a large, and unexpected, change. Even his newfound legislative clout was going to count for less than he had hoped. Not surprisingly, an unknown Republican opponent had appeared for 1974. Flynt's reaction was that "nobody is going to force me out. And just between you and me—off the record—I am going to beat the living hell out of this guy." The opponent was Newt Gingrich.

I had no contact with Jack Flynt during his 1974 reelection campaign. When we finished our interview in May 1974, I assumed—as he did—that he would be reelected without much difficulty. But that did not happen. He did not "beat the living hell" out of "this guy" Gingrich as he had predicted. He won by the skin of his teeth, with only 51 percent of the vote—by 2,774 votes out of 95,204 cast. In the face of change, he was barely holding on.

Looking back later, he described a casual, protectionist election effort in 1974 that was a carbon copy of what I had seen in 1970 and 1972. "I defeated him by a narrow margin because I didn't even campaign. I didn't realize that he had any support, any following, or that anybody knew him. I didn't even put out any literature, letters, or go visit anybody on a strictly campaign basis until about three weeks before the election. And I suddenly realized that he was making headway. So I got out and worked and won."[3] Flynt mounted no public campaign, and he spent only $33,000 to his opponent's $86,000.

When it was over, he did not know what had hit him. A family member who spent election night at his side watching the election results said, "He didn't say a word to me all night. He was ashen and in shock." When I phoned Flynt the next week to ask what happened, he shouted, "I damn near got my ass beat off, that's what happened!" And he turned me over to his top aide for further explanation.[4] Judging from this early reaction to the results, it appears that it had never occurred to the congressman that his new district required any altered electoral effort on his part.

In retrospect, it is clear that the uncertainties and the incapacities I had observed traveling with Flynt in 1972—the absence of a strenuous personal effort in the new part of the district and his interpretive bewilderment in suburbia—probably cost him dearly at the polls. The county-by-county vote patterns (see table 2) suggest that the incumbent was especially weak in suburbia. Flynt lost the new part of the district by 48 percent to 52 percent. And he lost the suburban counties of Clayton, Fulton, and Douglas combined by 47 percent to 53 percent. He had not succeeded in negotiating a mutually supportive representative relationship with his new constituents. His longtime person-intensive strategy had not served him well in the changed context.

Flynt survived in 1974, however, by carrying the other eleven counties (nine from his transitional district, and two from his new district) by 57 percent to 43 percent. The smaller the county, the more amenable it was to his representational strategy and the better he did. He had, in effect, met the challenge of his new district, in

Table 2. Georgia Sixth District Vote, 1974, by County

County	Flynt Vote %	Gingrich Vote %	Number of Votes
New District Counties plus Clayton			
Clayton	47	53	20,607
Douglas	47	53	6,569
Fulton (part)	47	53	24,291
Haralson	60	40	3,189
Jasper	78	22	1,127
Subtotal	48	52	55,783
Old District and Transitional District Counties			
Butts	72	28	2,011
Carroll[a]	46	54	9,232
Coweta	57	43	5,774
Fayette	51	49	3,933
Heard	74	26	1,006
Henry	59	41	5,366
Lamar	71	29	1,985
Pike	66	34	1,675
Spalding[b]	56	44	8,439
Subtotal	55	45	39,421
Total	51	49	95,204

[a] Gingrich's home county
[b] Flynt's home county

path-dependent fashion, by campaigning just the way he always had. And the relationship he had negotiated and maintained over the course of his long career had pulled him through a near-death experience. His expectation that the people who knew him personally or by his personal reputation would support him as strongly as ever was met in full.

1976, Day One: Catching Up

Buoyed by his near victory, challenger Gingrich announced that he would try again. And attracted by Jack Flynt's apparent vulnerability, three fellow Democrats announced for the 1976 primary against the incumbent. This time, Flynt could not possibly be surprised. The question was whether he would—or could—adapt to his new district more successfully in 1976 than in 1974. The strategic challenge had been made pretty clear in 1974. How would Flynt interpret it and cope with it? With that question in mind, I returned to the district in late October 1976, five days before election.

He had survived the Democratic primary in August with 58 percent of the vote in a four-way contest. When I asked him what he had done to help himself since 1974, he mentioned three things— "opening a district office in South Fulton, going home every weekend, and cultivating new friends without, in any way whatsoever, damaging my relations with my old friends." During the primary contest, a reporter had written that "people who've known Jack Flynt since his days as county prosecutor . . . say he is campaigning harder than at any time since first being elected to Congress." Flynt, he added, had emphasized "the things he can offer the voters which his opponents cannot: experience, service, legislative expertise, a proven record of fiscal responsibility," as well as the fact that he would "be the dean of Georgia's twelve-man delegation in Washington."[5] Flynt's primary opposition had moved him, for the first time since 1966, to produce a campaign brochure—in which he promised, "When elected, I'll be where I've always been, as close as a phone or a postage stamp." "That primary," Flynt said to me, "may have been the best thing that ever happened to me, because it sent me into the general election with a full head of steam."

Shortly after the primary, I was told, he had suffered a mild heart attack, and it worried him during my visit. On my second day there, he stopped at a medical clinic to see a doctor, saying, "Something felt funny a while ago." For the rest of that day, I drove the car. When he got home that evening, he went to the phone and called a friend. "I had a very uncomfortable day physically. I felt so bad I had a doctor check my heart and blood pressure. It all started Wednesday when I got up at 4:30 A.M. and got home at 12:30 A.M. I'm too old. I can't do that any more." Nevertheless, when I was there he kept up a fairly normal schedule of events—and filled in the gaps with energetic handshaking wherever he happened to be. For five days in late October, he campaigned about equally in the new and the old parts of the district.

The first event we attended was an after-dinner speech to forty Rotarians in his new area. It was, however, in small-town Haralson County, population 16,000. There, in the town of Bremen (population 3,900), Flynt's connections with his constituents mirrored those I had observed in my earlier visits. He began by identifying himself with his audience through personal, not policy, connections. "I went to grammar school and high school with a friend who lives six miles east of Buchanan on the road to Dallas," he said. "It is a joy to be with you because I am one of you."

Almost immediately, he moved to a new theme, his power in the House. He said he had not retired that year—as three of his Georgia colleagues had done—because, if elected, he could be of more service to his district than ever before as dean of the Georgia delegation and, in time, chairman of the Appropriations Committee. "If I become chairman of the Committee on Appropriations," he intoned, "the mantle will be draped, not only upon my shoulders, but upon the shoulders of every man, woman, and child in the Sixth District." Afterward he told me, "That [comment] was as close as I got to being political."

The remainder of his talk was a description of his new duties as chairman of the House Committee on Standards and Official Conduct (Ethics) and a discussion of its—and therefore his—importance in Congress. (He did not discuss any of the committee's specific activities, some of which had not played well in the Atlanta press.) The talk was, as usual, devoid of public policy discussions or legislative initiatives. The only two policy matters that were raised during the question period had nothing to do with his speech—one focused on the efficiency of the postal service, the other on the unionization of the armed services.

On the way home, Flynt named every person at every table and categorized each one as either a supporter (mostly) or a nonsupporter. Back home, he went right to the telephone to report to his top aide that "I had a good day [in Haralson County]. I went to Tallapoosa [population 2,600], Buchanan [population 1,089], and Bremen. I hope nobody will be upset because I couldn't see everybody. I went to see Owen Westbrook and Don Hawe. They were not there—but they'll know I came to see them."

Flynt's wife, Patty, had picked me up at the airport. And on the way to Bremen, we had "covered" a base in Haralson County's neighboring town, Villa Rica (population 3,400), by visiting with one of its leading citizens.[6] That visit, too, reflected the congressman's extraordinary concern for his one-on-one contacts, and his continual worry lest he fail to fulfill the representational expectations he had generated among his core supporters.

At home, Flynt stated flatly, "I'm in good shape. If I'm not, then

I'm missing the signs." He dwelled on the heartening signs in Clayton County. "South Fulton and Clayton," he said, "are the most important areas." Describing a Forest Park Rotary Club luncheon the day before, he said, "I'll bet 80 percent of them were for me." "Who were they?" I asked. "They were the more affluent, middle-class, upper-middle-class members of the community." He added that 275 people had come to another Clayton County event that evening. "All the best people in Clayton County," said his wife. He was cautiously pleased with these signs of his growing personal ties to local elites. "I got 40 percent of the vote [in the primary] in Clayton County. And if the vote had been counted qualitatively instead of quantitatively, I'd have won 80 percent. The quality people were with me. But every damn vote counts the same."

As for the great bulk of his new constituents—the "nonquality," non-elites—Flynt talked as if he had mounted a campaign to reach them. He had hired a campaign consultant, and he had taken two Washington staffers off his congressional payroll and put them on his campaign payroll. He had billboards up; he had mailed out 100,000 of his primary campaign brochures and distributed 10,000–20,000 more to various workers; he had one thirty-second positive television spot running, extolling his constituency service, his seniority, and his influence potential for the district; and he had just authorized an ad for district newspapers. "I told them to run the full page ad. I'm gonna win. After I win, I won't have the trouble raising the money."

As best as one can tell from his reports to the Federal Elections Commission, Flynt raised his money equally from individuals and from eighty political action committees (PACs). His campaign expenditures during the primary season emphasized billboards (primarily) and radio spots. As the campaign progressed, the bulk of the money went into television (primarily) and newspaper ads. The easiest spending categories to combine—because of the billing records—are television/radio and newspapers/billboards. In the first category, he spent about $37,000 (slightly more on television than on radio); in the second, he spent about $27,000 (slightly more on newspapers than billboards). With another $5,000 for brochures, posters, and photographs, his advertising budget was approximately $70,000— one-half of his total campaign budget.[7] All told, he spent $146,000 in 1976—four-and-a-half times more than in 1974.

1976, Day Two: Fayette County

My first full day on the campaign trail produced my newest and best evidence of Flynt's strategic challenge. We spent the day in Fayette County (population 20,000), once prototypically Old South, but now rapidly becoming prototypically New South. In 1958, for example, Fayette had registered the lowest percentage of its eligible black voters—1 percent—of any of Flynt's fifteen counties.[8] In the decade from 1960 to 1970, it had been—next to Clayton—the fastest-growing county in the district. In 1964 it had swung heavily (60 percent) for Barry Goldwater. The old and the new remained side by side, but the new was gaining. And Fayette County exemplified the challenge of the new.

Our itinerary began at Jackson Brothers, a general store in rural Woolsey. It took us, by way of Brooks, to the planned residential community of Peachtree City for some shopping-plaza campaigning and a luncheon talk at a country club. In the afternoon, we journeyed to the crossroads community of Starrs Mill, and then to the county seat, Fayetteville, for some person-to-person campaigning, followed by a speech at the all-candidate Fayette County Democratic Party rally.

The day did not begin well. The morning's *Atlanta Constitution* had endorsed Flynt's opponent.[9] "It ruined my breakfast," he said as we started out. But he quickly hit his stride. My notes describe the early morning coffee gathering at Jackson Brothers store.

When we got there, there were about a dozen pick-up trucks and five or six cars parked outside the one-room store with two gas pumps (none unleaded) out front. We went in, and there were about twenty men—all white, all over fifty-five, and one that looked eighty—standing around in bib overalls or pants and sport shirts of some kind. One man had on a coat and tie. They were sipping coffee and eating the cookies that were laid out on the counter. Overhead were all the yellowed cardboard displays of fishing tackle, sunglasses, nail clippers, etc. And right behind the cashier's spot, there were two shelves of packaged snuff. I counted sixteen varieties.

As soon as Jack had "howdied" with each one of the men, one brought out a paper bag and told Jack they had a present for him. Then they all gathered around, and when he had opened the bag, pulled out the wax-paper package inside, and opened the package,

Will Jackson said, "It's a Jimmy Carter sandwich, peanut butter and baloney." And they all guffawed and elbowed each other. Then, after a little more coffee and cookies, Will's brother, Robert Jackson, came out from the back of the store to shake hands with Jack. He had a buzzer in his hand so that when they shook hands, the buzzer tickled Jack's palm, and he jumped and laughed. That broke the boys up! "He shore jumped." "Yes he did." "He jumped right up." "He shore did."

As each additional customer came into the store, Jack would go over to say hello to them and say, "I hope you'll vote for me." Always, they said they would. (He spoke to each person individually. He did not speak to the group.)

Will Jackson took off his baseball-type cap and passed it around the group. Then he came over to me and said, "You're with Jack. Take the money. It'll buy him a little gas, won't it? Jack stays close to the people. He always stops in when he's going by. When he doesn't, he must be going awful fast and have something real important to do."

I said, yes, the money would help, and *he* could give it to Jack. "No, he's busy. You take it before some Republican gets his hands on it." So I did.

Then he said to me, "You come over here and have another cookie." And when I did, he said to me, "That old man standing over there is a Republican. He just is. The only one in the store. He says he'll vote for Jack, but not for Carter. Nobody can figure it out. I'm on the welfare board, and I know he's on welfare. Can you tell me why anybody on welfare would be a Republican?"

After some more howdying, Jack tucked a plug of Red Man tobacco in his cheek. Will, Jack, another man, and I left in two cars— those three in one, and me driving (Jack's car) behind them—to make "the rounds" (in Woolsey) of another store, the woodworking shop, and "our little hangout," which turned out to be the auto repair garage. Along the way, Jack might hop out and yell at somebody in a yard or driveway.

Then we all went to the tiny town of Brooks, where Jack went into the five or six stores on Main Street. In one of them, he bought some pepper sauce. As we left them to head toward Fayetteville, Will said, "Now you be sure to go around to the barbershop there. Gil said he hasn't seen you lately." Jack said, "I will. I may even get my hair cut." After saying goodbye and good luck, we left.

In the evening, when I recalled the experience at Jackson Brothers, the congressman looked at me, paused for effect, and said simply, "Dick, *those* are the people who elect me." He was not talking about the economically and/or politically influential elites of the county seats, like Thomaston and McDonough. He was talking about the less well-off, less well-educated, rural constituents who traditionally supported the Democratic candidate in the old, one-party South. Like the men in the store, many of these individuals, too, could think of their representative in terms of their personal contact with him.

The morning transition from the down-home atmosphere of Jackson Brothers country store to the upscale suburban ambience of Peachtree City was a cultural and a representational shock. The congressman, who connected so naturally with the first group of constituents, did not connect well with the second group. In Peachtree City's chic shopping plaza—with its art gallery and its interior decorating shop—he flew in and out of each store with a quick, "Hey, how you, how you doing? I'm Jack Flynt; I hope you will vote for me on Tuesday." He did not know a single one of these proprietors. Walking along outside, he handed out a few brochures. But he did not want me to help. I stood there as dozens and dozens of people walked by, oblivious to the candidate. Most of the other suburban campaigners I was studying would have had me handing out brochures hand over fist—for name recognition, if nothing else. But this congressman wanted personal contact or none at all.

Lunch at the Flat Creek Country Club—the only visit we ever made to a country club—was not Flynt's milieu either. He spoke woodenly. Afterward, he was upset because the old friend who had arranged the luncheon had failed to deliver any "important" new faces. "I know more people in Peachtree City than he does. He didn't have any of the right people at the luncheon." And he expressed his frustration with the community as a whole. "That goddamned Peachtree City," he said, "is the most anti-Carter [i.e., Republican] place I ever did see."

Fayette County was a comfortable commute to the nearby Atlanta Airport, and much of its growth was due to the influx of airline pilots and other well-paid employees of Delta and Eastern Airlines. (The blue-collar employees were more likely to settle in Clayton County.) In 1972 Flynt had emphasized how comfortable he felt with airline pilots. Now, however, he expressed frustration in connecting with these constituents. "Every airline pilot in the district is against me," he lamented as we drove toward Starrs Mill after lunch. "They are Republicans, I guess. No, I take that back—Ralph Presley is for me, Gene Weatherup is for me, Snake Smith is for me." He was cataloging the support of a huge occupational group individual by individual—as always. It was as if the category "airline pilots" was as easy to know and to deal with as the boys at Jackson Brothers or the Rotarians in Bremen. The pilots and other Fayette County newcomers could not, of course, be conceptualized by one-at-a-time thinking, nor could they be won over or represented by a person-intensive strategy. But that was Jack Flynt's way of thinking about representational connections, and he seemed bound by it.

The personal relationships he had previously developed remained, as always, impressively strong. After lunch we took a twenty-minute drive into the country, to the tiny crossroads area known as Starrs Mill, to visit for half an hour with the recently widowed proprietor of a little country store. Again, my notes describe the visit and my reaction to it.

We sat around a potbellied wood-burning stove (with a fire in it), Jack on a low, broken-down cane chair, I on a wooden chair, Mrs. Peeples on a stool. He gave her a big hug when he came in. She lost her husband (a county commissioner) six months ago. Jack came down [from Washington] for the funeral. And as she talked about her husband, she began to cry and sob—not out of control at all. She would get it under control and then get teary again. And Jack consoled her by recalling the good times.

She told how her husband loved watermelon and how they found him some—"I don't know where they found it"—on the day he died. "It was his last meal." And Jack said, "Do you remember that trip we all took to San Francisco?" And she said, "I sure do. I have some happy memories. I likes San Francisco. Some people say New Orleans is nice. I've never been there, but I sure likes San Francisco." It was so moving that I could hardly look at the two of them. She thanked him for taking time out to come see her and told him how hard it was to manage the farm and take care of the store. "I'm running across the road all day long." There were two black men waiting patiently (outside) for gasoline all the time we talked.

The point is that, here, in the midst of a campaign for his political life, Jack drove out of his way to go to this little fork in the road in the middle of nowhere to this tiny cinderblock store to console a woman in her grief. Most guys I know would have gone to a shopping center and "hit it" with a "brochure blitz" or something. Jack's friends are dying and he serves them to the end like his predecessors did seventy-five to 100 years ago. In that country store, it was just like it was in the 1800s. Nothing was going on in the outside world. A representative was just talking with his neighbor.

It was hardly a demonstration of up-to-date campaign efficiency. It was, instead, an up-to-date reminder of how deeply Jack Flynt valued and thrived upon his lifelong relationships with others.

In the afternoon we campaigned in Fayetteville—in and out of businesses and homes along Main Street—much as we had done in other years in other county seats. In the sheriff's office, the congressman shook hands all around. And the conversation reinforced his personal linkages.

Deputy: I heard you were over in Brooks this mornin'.
Flynt: I sure was.
Deputy: And you went by to see Mr. Larry Ford, didn't you?
Flynt: I sure did. And I stopped by at Mr. Putnam's and got me some pepper sauce.
Deputy: I know you did—that's a real fine pepper sauce.
Flynt: It sure is.
Deputy: You like pepper sauce, and ole Herman [Talmadge], he buys chewin' tobacco when he comes.

At the personal acquaintance level, Flynt's connections were secure. Wherever we stopped, people tendered their reassurances. "Would anyone tell you if there were soft spots?" I asked. "The last man we met in the bank would tell me," he answered. "If there were trouble, he'd draw me aside, take me into his office, close the door, and tell me who was falling off." And the banker had not done so.

When we visited in the home of a prominent, eighty-two-year-old lawyer friend down the street, however, Flynt's problem became clear. "Everything I hear is good," wheezed the lawyer. "Everybody I know says you're going to be alright, Jack." To which the congressman replied, "The trouble is that there are too many people moving in that you and I don't know." Flynt understood the problem; nonetheless, he spent an hour reminiscing in the drawing room of this highly respected, but very elderly man. "Why," I asked him, "are you campaigning mostly among your old friends?" "Most of them will vote for me," he said. "But now they'll go out and work a little harder."

The Democratic rally that evening gave no evidence of such hard work. It was a disaster. Thirty to forty people—mostly candidates—came. I recognized nearly all the noncandidates there, because they were the same old pals we had visited with during the day—Will Jackson, the banker, the lawyer. Flynt gave a perfunctory pro-Democratic, pro–Jimmy Carter speech. As soon as we got home, he phoned a campaign aide to complain bitterly about the pathetic party turnout. And he expressed a backward lament over the large micro-level effects of redistricting: "If they hadn't taken Troup, Meriwether, Bibb, Upson, Jones, and Monroe out of the district, I wouldn't be in a contest now."

Quite predictably, there was not—so far as I could recall from my notes—a single policy matter discussed anywhere all day. At home that evening, one of his children asked me, "How come issues don't seem to matter in Georgia? I always thought [the reason was] that if you gave the kind of personal service Pop does, you had to neglect the other parts of your job. When people ask me, 'How come Flynt doesn't have his name on a piece of legislation?,' I always tell them that it's the personal service that's the most important part of the job, and that's what they get from him. Is it possible for members to handle issues and personal service at the same time?" The answer, of course, was yes. But Jack Flynt's commitments were heavily loaded on one side of that equation.

I summarized in my notes: "Each night when he comes home, he tells Patty news about everyone he has met. It seems important to him—who he ate with, what they said to him, what news they exchanged. There is a continuous stream of personal comments, but none—never, never, never—anything about the issues of the day. He has opinions on these, if asked. But these were not the stuff of today's speeches or conversations."

My further notebook ruminations describe my overall observations, impressions, and conclusions from our day in Fayette County.

While from a political scientist's standpoint, what I am watching is fascinating, I feel sad at what I am watching. For one can see time passing Jack by. . . . He may win. He continues to think so. . . . Even if he does win, it is sad to see that he is unable to cope with the new district he has been given. It was a day in which he campaigned in his person-to-person style effectively and—in the case of Mrs. Peeples, the widow in the country store—movingly. But he is going through the same motions with the same old people in the same old way in a district that is fast-changing, younger, mobile, less Democratic than before. . . . The sadness I feel is magnified because his attachment to the people who are his strongest supporters is the kind of attachment the Founding Fathers surely had in mind. It is personal, whole, and genuine. But it cannot last in large districts. . . . Person-to-person campaigning cannot survive a great reshuffling of people. It is built up over a long period of time, and it produces a highly personal trust. To watch him fumble in Peachtree City after the morning at the country store was almost like you were watching time-lapse photography in which 100 years of American history was collapsed into two hours. Jackson Brothers was how southern rural politics was conducted for 100 years, [and] Peachtree City is the milieu of today. . . . Jack is a throwback to a simpler time . . . [that] is gone, and he is going with it—if not this time, then before long. The next congressman will not be a Jack Flynt nor anyone chosen by him. It's a little like watching the last train run through town.

As these notes make clear, I certainly wanted that last train to complete its journey successfully.

1976, Campaign Problems

The signs surrounding Flynt's conventional campaign efforts were not positive, however. In the beginning, for example, he had not wanted a brochure at all, his staffers said. And when he finally agreed, he wanted one "just like" the one in 1966. The campaign, I was told, had had no luck recruiting volunteers. Volunteers are attracted by issues, and the only issue position Flynt had included in his brochure was his opposition to gun control. Sometimes volunteers came, the staffers told me, but they did not come back. Many were young people, and the congressman, they feared, had trouble relating to young people.

Driving home from Bremen at about nine o'clock, we had seen Flynt's Coweta County headquarters in Newnan standing empty and dark; nearby, his opponent's headquarters was ablaze with light and full of people. It was not a heartening scene, but Flynt had made no comment. In the end there were, at most, half-a-dozen people doing all the day-to-day campaign drudgery. And they did not always complete their tasks. I noted that when we stopped at a local party headquarters or at supporters' homes, large quantities of Flynt's brochures were lying about in unpacked bundles. Not surprisingly, the congressman had taken no polls. As always, Jack Flynt remained largely a one-man band. In no sense did he have a modern campaign organization.

On the trail, another campaign problem surfaced: his disastrous relations with the most influential newspaper in his district—more influential now, in the new district, than in the old one. The *Atlanta Constitution* had opposed Flynt in 1974 but had supported him in the 1976 Democratic primary.[10] Now the paper was opposing him again, arguing that he had not been sufficiently aggressive as Ethics Committee chairman and was "not in the best of health." Both arguments were designed to frame the overall debate, as Gingrich had framed it, as the old politics versus the new politics. Because of the primary endorsement, Flynt said, "I thought they'd do what the *Atlanta Journal* did, endorse neither of us."

The day after the paper's endorsement of Gingrich, a *Constitution* cartoon pictured Flynt as a fat politician trying to exorcise his political skeletons from a graveyard. And the Sunday edition featured an anti-Flynt editorial cartoon depicting him as a bloated windbag, telling his youthful opponent that "Smear . . . distortion . . . prevarication is part of campaigning, son!" Aides described it as a "vendetta," and Flynt agreed that the newspaper's editors had "always" opposed him because he was "too conservative" for them. After the election he expressed his opinion that "they did everything they could possibly do to defeat the man within the Georgia delegation who can do more than anyone else to make sure that the Carter administration is a great one. I wanted to tell them that. I don't know whether they did it out of vindictiveness or misinformation, but their attack on me . . . was the most vicious attack I have ever experienced in my life." It was not a helpful campaign relationship.

Another drag on the Flynt campaign was the new partisan context, with the national Republican Party giving a great deal of help to its candidate while the national Democratic Party was giving none to its southern conservative candidate.[11] "The Republicans," said Flynt, "want to defeat me almost as much as the *Atlanta Constitution* does."

He was particularly upset at the Republican president, Gerald Ford. "He's an ungrateful SOB. He could have stopped this guy from running against me, or at least stopped the Republicans from sending in $50,000 to beat me. I've supported more of his vetoes than most Republicans. But all he cares about is selfish partisan advantage. He did the same thing in 1966, campaigned against me. . . . He is not loyal to his friends." Flynt's voting record cut no ice with a Republican Party intent on increasing its congressional strength in the South.

Moreover, the congressman was at odds with his own presidential candidate. Flynt had been enthusiastic about Jimmy Carter in 1970, but he had come to hold the Georgia governor responsible for the damaging 1972 redistricting—not to mention Carter's "destruction of the Flint River dam complex" and his antisegregation sentiments. "I'm the only Democratic candidate in the country that Jimmy Carter did not congratulate after my primary—no, Larry MacDonald, too."[12] Self-preservation, however, demanded that Flynt campaign for Carter and hope to ride his coattails. "What else can I do?" he said. In his relations with the two national parties, the southern conservative was being whipsawed into a partisan no man's land where he was left very much on his own.

One small change in this campaign was the appearance, for the first time, of an expressed interest in black voters. All the 1976 relationships discussed so far were with white people. But the new district had brought Flynt a more active black electorate in the area of South Fulton, closest to the city of Atlanta. "It's a middle-class black area," he said. "Twenty percent of the Atlanta police force is black, and 80 percent of them live in my new district." With the prospect of a close election looming, and with a Georgian with strong ties to the black community at the top of the ticket, a new set of strategic calculations came into play. Every black vote, he knew, would be a Carter vote. But in the Georgia voting booth, he explained, "you have to vote twice. I hope they will vote for me, too."

For the first time, I saw Flynt soliciting votes, one by one, among black constituents. I watched him shake hands with eight women making barbecue in a large restaurant. ("Do you want to shake hands with the blacks in the kitchen?" "I sure do.") For the first time, I saw him shaking hands among a dozen or so nonplussed black students at Clayton Junior College. "Hey, I'm Jack Flynt. How you? How you doin? Ah hope you have a nice day, and ah hope you'll help me have a nice day next Tuesday." A recent event at the home of a black contractor, Patty Flynt told me, was "the first time we have *ever* been together, to any gathering, where we were the only white people there." At that party, said Jack, "I told them that if I was reelected, I was going to take [the contractor's daughter] back with me to Washington"—a first for his staff.

He expressed pleasure that the young woman in question had worked for him in the campaign. "Some of my redneck friends criticized me when she worked with me knocking on doors in College Park." Several times, he told a story about Gingrich spotting this young woman and her father at some event and saying (according to the contractor), "What's that black chick doing working for Flynt? What has he ever done for black people?" Whereupon her father had come up behind Gingrich, tapped him on the shoulder (here, Flynt would turn me around so he could tap me on the shoulder to dramatize the moment), and said to him, "I'm her father, and what have *you* ever done for black people?"

The notion that Flynt might be engaged in a competition for black constituent support was one novelty of his campaign performance.[13] It was the first visible political impact I had yet encountered of the civil rights revolution in the Sixth District. That huge turning point in national politics was filtering into individual House districts incrementally and at very different rates of speed.

1976, Final Days

On the third evening of my visit, incumbent and challenger met in their one face-to-face debate. It was the only time I saw the challenger, in whom I had no interest. Flynt spoke of him only occasionally and briefly("I'm running against an absolute idiot. The trouble is, he's an educated idiot"). He did not like Newt Gingrich. When pressed to do more television debates, he declined, saying, "When you lie down with dogs, you get up with fleas."[14] As we would expect, this dislike had nothing whatever to do with public policy. Flynt did not think of Gingrich in terms of public policy differences. His dislike was entirely personal.

He saw his opponent as a person who was not embedded in the community, who was not "one of us," and who could not, therefore, be a good representative of the constituency. He buttressed this view with the argument that Gingrich had not been born, raised, or educated in Georgia. Gingrich's election, said Flynt, "would be a tragedy for the people of the Sixth District. . . .Let's hope we send him outside the state of Georgia." Flynt also saw his opponent in a purely competitive sense, as a person who was dedicated to pushing the "king" off his hill—and he had never liked anyone who pushed him. Moreover, Gingrich was attacking him in the most personal terms— and on a prototypical suburban issue, ethics. Gingrich accused Flynt of lax ethical standards at home for leasing land to the Ford Motor Company while voting against clean air legislation, and for foot dragging as Ethics Committee chairman in pursuing the Koreagate investigation.[15] By the time of the debate, the very sighting of an "Elect Gingrich" sign along the roadside triggered both competitive juices and choice epithets.

He made no special preparations for his one television debate with his opponent. Early that day, he campaigned (in the pouring rain) in the stores of two South Fulton County towns, Fairburn and Union City. From there he went to the hospital to visit a sick friend, then to a funeral parlor to pay respects to another friend who had died the day before in a plane crash, then to that same friend's home to console his wife, then to another hospital to look in on the three survivors of that plane crash, and, finally, to the dedication of a new control tower at the airport.

It was a typical Flynt day—person to person. And it produced one story that captured its limitations. Driving from the airport through the Clayton County town of Morrow, the congressman commented instructively on its mayor: "I gave the town a flag that I bought myself when they dedicated the flagpole. And that son of a bitch turned around one day later and made a contribution to my opponent." Otherwise, Flynt was absorbed and noncommunicative. He went to the debate straight from the airport—without any practice, any memos, any talking points, or any coaching.

In response to Gingrich's opening attack on him as an exemplar of all that was bad in a discredited Congress, Flynt adopted a classic anti-Congress stance, disassociating himself from the institution. "I do not accept responsibility for any actions of Congress. I do not want to be tarred with the brush being applied to other members of Congress. I want to be judged on how well Jack Flynt has done, what Jack Flynt has said, and what service Jack Flynt has given to the people of the Sixth District of Georgia."

Though Gingrich had campaigned as a Rockefeller Republican and had been supported by the *Atlanta Constitution* as a "liberal"—

and was supported, too, by environmental, education, and labor groups—the only direct policy clash I noted occurred over amnesty for draft evaders. On that issue, Flynt clearly took the harder line, tailored, he said, to the views of his constituents. For me, however, the message of the debate had nothing to do with policy.

What the debate did was to make very clear yet another aspect of Flynt's representational challenge—the increasing importance of the media and his problems in adapting to it. The medium—television—was the message of the debate. And the lessons of the debate were visual. Flynt seemed to understand. Afterward, he was concerned only with "Did I look well on television?" and "Did I look strong?" Everyone said he had.

My private reaction is best conveyed in my notes.

The debate was a real eye-opener for me. I do not know Gingrich, and would not want to jump to any conclusions, but the young, media-oriented candidate was there, presented (except for a squeaky voice) to perfection. His hair and dress were immaculate. His debating style was Kennedyesque—the jabbing fingers, the use of statistics, the quickness at parry and thrust.

When Jack said he was glad to be endorsed by Frank Bailey [his primary opponent] and Senator Talmadge, Gingrich said he was not claiming endorsements by any working politicians, only "the people." ([Barry] Goldwater, [John] Connally, [John] Rhodes all came in to endorse *him*.) But I thought it was his best score in his effort to depict Jack as part of the old, tired, leaderless system of government. Jack looks like an old-time southern politician. If I had been a Gingrich backer, I'd have been pleased by the contrast—the nattily dressed, articulate young man side-by-side with the old bull.

But what "disturbs" me is that I know that when Jack talks about service, he means real service to real people. What I cannot tell is whether Gingrich is or is not as genuinely compassionate as Jack is. He may be. If he is, fine. If he's not, then the system we now have gives enormous advantages to the media candidate. For it is amply clear that Gingrich can manipulate the local press beautifully. Everything is pro-Gingrich. One [former] editor is his press secretary. Another editor was his press secretary last time . . .

He cannot "know" [his supporters] the way Jack "knows" his supporters. But he can win their vote via the media—without seeing them or feeling them or touching them. Jack does things the old way. He has whole relationships with people . . . but his methods are not appropriate to the society in which he finds himself—the society of change and impermanence. . . . In sum, I thought the TV program presented a choice for the voters—the young "candidate" (à la Redford) and the old politician. The voters have a style choice and we'll see.

The debate marked the effective end of the Flynt campaign—and left no mark on it. For the remainder of my visit, the congressman marked time.

On my last day, I asked him to rank some of the campaign activities I had witnessed, first, according to their political importance for him, and second, according to how comfortable he felt in each setting. His rankings are shown in table 3.

As Flynt saw it, the most important activities were those in which he pursued his protectionist strategy, reinforcing the loyalty of people he had represented for so long. And those same activities were, by and large, the ones that were most comfortable for him—the Bremen Rotary Club, Jackson Brothers general store, the nearby rural areas. Conversely, the least important activities were, by and large, expansionist in nature and least comfortable for him. Those activities included the multiperson, formal events in the suburbanized part of the district—the luncheon, the rally, and vote gathering in Peachtree City. Other activities ranked in between, with the debate more important than comfortable, and Clayton Junior College more comfortable than important. The first discrepancy is understandable, but Flynt's personal comfort at Clayton is inexplicable. Perhaps it was the total lack of pressure accompanying this make-work, day-before-election activity or the simple fact that it was one on one.

Jack Flynt's choice of a person-intensive representational strategy "came early and stayed late." The contours of his choice had become pretty clear by the end of my first visit in 1970. But I could not have known then how much the range of possible strategies had already been narrowed to exclude all others. Nor could I have known that as I fleshed out and confirmed my tentative conclusion during my second visit. Only in the changed and challenging circumstances of my third visit did I come to realize that in fact Flynt's choice of representational strategies had been foreclosed by the sequential developments—and the unbroken electoral successes—of his long

Table 3. Flynt Rankings of Campaign Activities, 1976

Activity (in Sequence)	Political Importance	Personal Comfort
Rotary Club speech, Bremen	1	2
Campaign coffee, Jackson Brothers store (near Woolsey)	2	1
Campaigning, Woolsey, Brooks, Starrs Mill	3	4
Luncheon, Flat Creek Country Club, Peachtree City	9	9
Campaigning, Peachtree City shopping plaza	8	8
Campaigning, Fayetteville	6	7
Democratic Party rally, Fayetteville	10	10
Campaigning, Union City, Fairburn (South Fulton) shopping plazas	5	5
Debate with opponent, WSB-TV	4	6
Campaigning, Clayton Junior College	7	3

career, and by the accumulation of personal negotiations over years of personal engagement with his supportive constituents. By 1976 he had no options. He was constrained by his past; he could not change. He would campaign with a person-to-person style, predicated on a person-intensive representational strategy. For better or worse, challenged or not, he would do, in path-dependent fashion, what he had always done.

1976, Election Results

Jack Flynt was reelected by a margin of 5,132 votes out of 149,866 cast, or 52 percent to 48 percent, a slight statistical improvement over his 1974 results. His county-by-county vote percentages, ordered from the largest to the smallest, are shown in column 1 of table 4. To establish some sense of Flynt's county-based strength, the size of the actual 1976 electorate in each county, ordered from smallest to largest, is shown in column 2.

A comparison of the two columns is strongly supportive of the notion that Flynt's political strength lay in his smaller, nonsuburban counties. There is a substantial, eyeball correlation between the size of his victory and the size of the electorate. The clusters of counties in the top halves of the two columns look a lot alike. That is, the smaller a county's electorate—and, therefore, the stronger Flynt's personal connections—the greater his electoral margin. Since most

Table 4. Flynt County Strengths, 1976

County Ranking by Flynt Vote %		County Ranking by Size of Electorate	
County	%	County	Electorate
Butts	76	Heard	1,912
Jasper	75	Jasper	2,039
Heard	75	Pike	2,573
Pike	68	Lamar	3,248
Lamar	67	Butts	3,344
Haralson	67	Haralson	5,213
Coweta	59	Fayette	6,386
Spalding[a]	59	Henry	7,606
Henry	57	Coweta	9,043
Fulton (part)	50.1	Spalding[a]	10,562
Carroll[b]	49	Douglas	10,896
Clayton	44	Carroll[b]	13,789
Fayette	42	Clayton	33,896
Douglas	41	Fulton (part)	39,359

Note: The county vote percentages are arranged from the largest to the smallest, whereas the size of the electorate figures are arranged from the smallest to the largest.
[a] Flynt's home county
[b] Gingrich's home county

of the small counties were in his old district, it is clear that he held his base of strength there. Among the counties in his new district, he won strong support in the two small ones that were most like those in his old district (Jasper and Haralson). In other words, where the context allowed for a person-intensive campaign and a person-intensive representational strategy, Jack Flynt remained as successful as ever.

Table 4 also reveals his troubles in the larger, suburban parts of the old district (that is, in Clayton) and in the suburban part of the new district (Douglas). The major anomaly in the orderings is Fayette County—small in size, but anti-Flynt in sentiment. Fayette is the county where my narrative pictures him as deeply attached to people in Old South communities like Woolsey, but unable to connect with the rapidly expanding population in New South communities like Peachtree City. (The other anomaly, Fulton County, will be discussed shortly.)

To help us see the world as Flynt saw it, I asked him, three days

Table 5. Flynt Predictions and Election Results, 1976

County	Predicted Vote %	Actual Vote %	% Difference
Butts	65	76	+11
Carroll	40	49	+9
Heard	70	75	+5
Fulton	48	50	+2
Spalding	60	59	−1
Lamar	70	67	−3
Jasper	80	75	−5
Pike	75	68	−7
Henry	67	57	−10
Clayton	55	44	−11
Fayette	55	42	−13
Coweta	—	59	—
Douglas	—	41	—

before the election, to predict his vote percentage in each county. Comparing his predictions with the actual results gives us some indication of how closely in touch he was with the voters in different counties. Table 5 presents that comparison, with counties arrayed top to bottom—from those where he did better than he expected to those where he did worse than he expected.

Not surprisingly, his "best" prediction, that is, the county he appeared to know best of all, came in his home county, Spalding. Not surprisingly, either, his expectations were met least well in Fayette and Clayton Counties—along with two other counties, Butts and Henry, that did not stand out before.

I took these predictions and results with me when I conducted a brief postmortem with Flynt three weeks after the election. Once again, we found a substantial contrast between his electorally strong counties and his electorally weak ones—between counties in which his representational strategy worked and those where it did not. His lifelong emphasis on personal relationships appears to have been as central to his political thinking as ever.

The results in Clayton, his long-neglected outlier, remained beyond his capacity to understand. His preelection prediction there was way off the mark. "It was an absolute shocker to me," he said. "I don't know what I could have done to change it. We put in more effort there than anywhere—day or night. We even knocked on doors. What happened, I do not know."

In Fayette County, he had made an even more egregious overestimate of his strength. And this newly suburbanizing county was as much a puzzle as wholly suburbanized Clayton. "It was a disaster," said Flynt, "almost as bad as Clayton. [It was actually worse.] A lot of it was because I had the wrong man actively associated with me. Whether that accounted for a switch of 500 votes one way and 500 the other, I don't know. You remember that rally we had on Friday before the Tuesday election? That was an absolute disaster. The man who ran it didn't know what he was doing and made no effort to coordinate with the other candidates." It is not surprising that Flynt should try to find a person-related explanation. But it was his dependence upon this out-of-touch supporter that was the proximate problem. Fayette was the fastest growing, after Clayton, of the fifteen counties in his original district, and it was, for that reason, the first to grow out of touch with him. He remarked later, with respect to one litmus group, that "there are 1,500 airplane pilots in my district, and I'll bet not more than ten voted for me. They just vote Republican. They didn't know I was the more conservative man in the race."

Henry County was another suburban county where population change may explain Flynt's overly optimistic prediction. "It was a disappointment to some," he said, "but it's a changing population county, so I was pleased with it."

I never saw him in his new suburban county, Douglas. But it looked like he had not been able to cultivate it successfully in the years since 1972. When making his predictions, he had commented, "About Douglas County—I can't say one thing about how we're going to do. They have the third largest number of voters behind Fulton and Clayton. I don't know what they will do." True to his words, he made no prediction.

In counties where he did better than expected, Flynt credited his strong, longtime supporters. In Butts: "I did better than expected because of local organizers and professionals who knew what they were doing—some of them people whom I have known for twenty-five years." In Carroll: "This was a vast improvement over two years ago, largely because of a heavy concentration of effort by me and by local people who were identifiable Democrats." And in Jasper: "Last time, I got eighty percent in Jasper. I fell off. But 75 percent isn't bad. Here again, there was a local effort by professionals—people I have known and people they know." It was his way of saying that a person-intensive representational strategy was the foundation of his winning campaign strategy.

The strategy was successful, of course, only among his white supporters, not among the district's black voters. Ironically, however, the overwhelming support of his black constituents—particularly the ones who were new to him and did not know him—probably accounted for Flynt's margin of victory. In eight predominantly black precincts in South Fulton, he ran ahead of his Republican opponent by 4,688 votes. And the other 445 votes of his victory margin could easily have been made up by black voters in areas adjacent to the South Fulton area. Turnout in the eight precincts was 68 percent ahead of the 1974 turnout. Over 50 percent of the registered voters in those precincts had turned out to support the Democrat they knew, Jimmy Carter, and in the voting booth, they pulled the lever for the Democratic congressional candidate, too. In the eight black precincts, Flynt's vote ranged from a low of 76 percent to a high of 93 percent, for an impressive overall margin of 86 percent. He polled 5,575 votes overall to his opponent's 887. It was a vote performance that rivaled his all-time highs elsewhere.

Jack Flynt's black constituents had pulled the congressional lever for a representative who had voted against every civil rights bill and every voting rights bill put before him. It was a dramatic example of the possible disconnect between winning and representing. Flynt had won, but he had never represented the essential interests of the very people who probably gave him the margin of his victory.

His 50.1 percent in South Fulton was better than he had predicted. His reaction, however, was quite matter-of-fact, as if he had known all along that he would benefit from Carter support among black voters. "The black vote was heavier than usual, and it went 80 percent to 90 percent for me," he said. "I was disappointed in some of the outlying [white] areas in the county. I thought I could carry them. We lost some precincts there that we didn't feel we should have, but the black turnout compensated for them."

An *Atlanta Journal and Constitution* analysis of the unincorporated areas of South Fulton showed considerable ticket splitting among heavily white suburbanites there—pro-Carter, anti-Flynt.[16] So I asked him, "How much do you attribute your vote to Jimmy Carter?" "About fifty-fifty," Flynt replied. "He ran stronger in the district than I did. He got some young people I lost. But I picked up some older people that he lost. My margin in the district was greater than his margin in the country." Victory margins, of course, can be found anywhere among various clusters of supporters. Jack Flynt was not about to locate his own narrow victory margins among the black members of his reelection constituency—or on the coattails of Jimmy Carter. A reasonable analysis, however, suggests otherwise.

Retirement

Immediately after the election, Flynt announced his intention to run for reelection in 1978.[17] Two months later he decided, privately, that he would not. And a year later, in February 1978, in three terse sentences, he announced his retirement.[18] He declined to elaborate for the press.

"I couldn't announce it earlier," he said when we talked in March 1978. "If you do that, you become a lame duck and lose whatever power you had around here. . . . Actually, I had thought of retiring for the last six years. Each time there was speculation among my enemies about my retirement. I didn't want them retiring me. So I stayed on." But, he added, another incentive had been the fading hope of Appropriations Committee leadership.

When I asked him, "Why now?," he put his hand over his head and said, "Because I've had it up to here, that's why. I can't put up with all the crap you have to take around here. The job is too much trouble. That's a strong statement, I know. It wasn't true twenty years ago; it wasn't true ten years ago. But it is now. I think I could have won again. But what's the sense of beating your damn brains out to get somewhere when there's no pleasure in it after you get there?"

"What has changed?" I asked. "That's a hard question to answer," he responded, "and I'll try to get one for you. A *New York Times* reporter called and asked me for thirty minutes sometime between now and next Wednesday to talk about my retirement. I told him that if I had thirty minutes to give him, I wouldn't be retiring. I thought that was a pretty good answer." He was saying that his Washington job had changed. His Ethics Committee chairmanship had brought him more inside work and more outside criticism. And he admitted, "My health is not as good as it was when I was thirty-nine. I can feel that I've put on some years since I was in the hospital with my heart attack." More demands and less energy was not an inviting pair of circumstances.

Flynt expressed particular disappointment in his relations with President Carter. In November 1976 he had characterized the relationship, publicly and optimistically, as "a lasting and ever-strengthening friendship."[19] It had been anything but that, however.

> Would you believe it if I told you that my relations with the president had something to do with my retirement? He's the first president ever from Georgia. He's the first president ever from the Southeast. Yet he and I disagree on almost everything. It's as if he was pointing toward the magnetic South Pole and I was pointing toward the magnetic North Pole. I'm the dean of the Georgia delegation, the Georgian with the longest service in Congress. I should be out there leading the charge for his legislation. But he has hardly sent up anything I can support. . . . He's the most antibusiness president we've had in the history of this country.

For a man to whom the Georgia delegation had always been a refuge within an increasingly liberal national party, a man who, in 1976, had touted his accession to the delegation's leadership, it was a great disappointment that the achievement had brought him neither plea-sure nor influence.

Although I pressed him on the problem of increased competition back in the district, Flynt declined to accept it as a factor in his retirement—except to acknowledge that from then on, he would always have had an opponent, as well as less time to spend in the district. When I put the problem of Clayton, South Fulton, and Douglas to him, he repeated his sense of frustration. "There's no way on God's earth that anyone can represent them. They are too tran-sient in their domiciles and in their thoughts to let anybody represent them for long. If they put a man in, they'll be the very ones to turn him out." It was an uninviting prospect. And while he later said of Gingrich, "If I had run again in 1978, I think I would have beaten the living daylights out of him," he did not put that thought to the test. Given the contextual challenges that lay ahead for a person-intensive representational strategy, it was most probably a prudent decision.

Knowing why Jack Flynt was attracted to politics in the beginning helps us understand why he retired from politics at the end. He got into politics to enjoy the individual contacts and the community participation associated with service to others. As both campaigning and governing became increasingly strenuous, demanding, and difficult, however, the opportunities for maintaining his accustomed level of personal satisfaction diminished.[20] Of course, the possibility of increased institutional influence remained. But that was never a compelling goal for him, nor was the achievement within "striking distance."[21] Flynt got into politics because he loved politics, but the kind of politics he loved was becoming less tenable for him. So he left. Whether a policy-driven representative might have stayed longer and fought harder is an open question. But for Jack Flynt, in his time and place, political change had seriously undermined the motivational foundations of his public career.

Throughout the Jack Flynt story, there is a tacit assumption that person-intensive strategies of representation could be found in other southern districts during the same period. I present no supporting evidence. But if "Old South" refers to distinctive socioeconomic and political patterns, and if the political career of Jack Flynt was embedded in and was responsive to those patterns, it is very likely that the representational activities of some other southern House members would look very much like his.

On the other hand, I do not mean to imply that other representational strategies could not be found in the South. To the contrary, there were southern Democrats whose public profiles, at least, suggested a driving interest in affecting—even changing—major public policies. Representatives Carl Elliott from Alabama and Frank Smith from Mississippi, on racial policy, come to mind. In their representational choices, they were, indeed, harbingers of the New South, and their contrasts with Jack Flynt—in constituency negotiations and congressional career—would make for a fascinating comparative study.[22] But they were in a distinct minority among their southern Democratic colleagues. And both were eventually defeated by fellow Democrats. It fell, therefore, to the southern Republicans to bring a fresh and dominating cohort of policy-driven politicians into the House of Representatives.

CHAPTER FOUR

Mac Collins, 1996–1998

A Policy-Intensive Strategy

Introduction

In the years following Jack Flynt's retirement, a voluminous literature appeared on "the transformation of Southern politics"[1] and on
"the equally important transformations of the region's population,
economy and social structure."[2] Curiosity about what might have
happened to House member-constituency relationships led me to
return to Flynt's territory in early 1996 to travel with one of his
successors. Mac Collins had been elected in 1992 and reelected in
1994. Three-quarters of his constituents lived within the boundaries
of Flynt's 1976 district; in 1996 a court-ordered redistricting reduced
that overlap to two-thirds. So, while the geographical constituencies
of the two representatives were not a perfect match, they were close
enough to encourage comparison. And there was obviously enough
change to sustain a comparative inquiry. Indeed, the simple fact that
the district had traded a Democratic congressman for a Republican
congressman was sufficient to that end.

My expectation was that any changes I observed could be explained by some combination of individual, contextual, and sequencing factors. And my argument will be that this combination of factors
will help us account for an observable change in representational
strategy from the person-intensive strategy of Jack Flynt to the policy-
intensive strategy of Mac Collins.

Individual and Goals

When I returned to Georgia in February 1996, Michael (Mac) Collins was fifty-two years old, in his fourth year in Congress and his twelfth year in elective office. Born and raised in Flovilla in Butts County, Collins was a graduate of Jackson High School and founder of the Collins Trucking Company.[3] His career milestones included unsuccessful runs (as a Democrat) for the Butts County Commission in 1974 and 1975; election as chairman of the Butts County Commission from 1977 to 1980; defeat for reelection to the county commission in 1980; election as Butts County Republican Party chairman from 1981 to 1983, after switching parties in 1981; unsuccessful runs for the Georgia state senate in 1984 and 1986; election to the Georgia state senate from 1989 to 1993; election to the U.S. Congress in 1993; and appointment to the House Committee on Ways and Means in 1995.

There were obvious career differences from Jack Flynt. Collins was a businessman, not a career politician. His political career had not been one of unbroken success. And Collins was at a much earlier stage of his career in Congress when we met.

There were also similarities between the two politicians. Collins, too, was a local boy, raised in a politically and electorally oriented family. "My mother was a member of the city council of our small community of Flovilla [population 284 in 1960]. When I was a small boy, I would hear her come in and talk about council meetings. She was in charge of roads and parks. As boys, we would cut the grass for the city. She enjoyed her job. My daddy always wanted to be a county commissioner, but he never did run. My father had a third-grade education. My mother had a fifth-grade education. I felt that if they wanted to be in politics, then, gosh, I did, too." This combination of local roots and family approval may help account for another Flynt/Collins similarity—that both men have thought of politics as a worthwhile and honorable profession. Unlike many of their colleagues, I never heard either one complain about the political life he had chosen or denigrate the institution to which he belonged.

The biggest personal difference between them was that Collins had a relevant prepolitical career.[4] He was a successful businessman. From the time he mowed grass for the city in order to buy his first automobile, Collins literally worked his way into politics. His family could not give him the early preferment—a private-school secondary education and college—that Flynt's family had provided. During and after high school, he worked as a truck driver. At the age of eighteen, he organized a company that became, when he was twenty-five, the Collins Trucking Company.[5] It thrived by hauling logs for Georgia Pacific and eventually grew to a fleet of thirty-seven trucks. For twenty years Collins also owned a Chevrolet dealership, and for ten years he co-owned a half-dozen grocery stores. As of 1998 only trucking remained. Less than five minutes after we met, he said, "I'm not your typical Ivy League congressman. I come from the school of hard knocks. I've spent my whole life close to working people."

Collins won his first office, Butts County commissioner, as a businessman reformer. As the Democratic chairman of the commission, he brought business practices to outdated county government. "When we took over," he recounted, "the county had no money—only enough for one payroll. The roads were in terrible shape, and it was the middle of winter. Do you know how the good old boys made up the county budget? They just added 10 percent to the previous year's budget. I was very aggressive on budgets, spending, and roads. One rainy day, I went out to check on some road work and I found them all sitting inside having coffee. They said they didn't work in the rain. I told them that in my trucking company, we always work in the rain and that they would in the county, too."

He also successfully pushed to abolish the long-standing system under which the county clerk of court and the county tax commission kept a percentage of all the fees they collected. "It was a system that had long out-lived its usefulness and had possibilities for wrongdoing," he recalled. But it cost him. "I was defeated at the next election by a 'get even' vote." And these "bad feelings," he says, cost him one more defeat—in his first state senate race. But he persisted.

Mac Collins, like Flynt, exhibited his political ambition by climbing a three-step electoral ladder from smaller to larger constituencies—in this case, from county- to state- to national-level office. But along the way, he lost as many campaigns as he won. His persistence in the face of multiple electoral defeats can be explained partly by his willingness to take risks in pursuit of all his goals, and partly by the special force of his policy goals.

He certainly took risks to achieve his policy goals. Why, I asked, did he challenge, in 1988, a sitting state senator who had already beaten him once?

He was a former Superior Court judge. He had edged me out at 49.3 percent two years earlier. It was a hard battle. I had said I was not going to run again. But he was opposed to the death penalty. He got on the Judiciary Committee, and he got a bill passed providing that no one with an IQ less than seventy could be sentenced to death. Prior to the bill's passage, seven members of a family were murdered by three prison escapees. They were caught, pleaded guilty, and were sentenced to death. When two of them scored below seventy on the IQ test, they escaped the death penalty. That did not settle well with folks. Still, everyone told me I could not win against an incumbent and a former judge. I said, "I will. I'm going to make one more try, and I'm going to beat him on his bill." I focused on what he focused on—crime. I explained his record on crime. And I won, by 52 or 53 percent.

Collins came to the state senate as a law and order representative. He served in the minority there—as a "crusty and outspoken dissident"— for four years. As he explained it, "I don't like playing defense."[6]

In the congressional election of 1992, Collins was not the insiders' favorite nominee, nor was he favored to win when he became the nominee. His prospective congressional district had been drawn to be safely Democratic.[7] His home had been carved out of it as a discouragement, and a Democratic incumbent was running there. Yet he triumphed in both the primary and the general election. Why did he persist? He explained at the time that, in working for state and local government, "you see that the real policy comes out of Washington, D.C. If you object to some of that policy, you've got to go where the policy is made. And that's Washington, D.C."[8]

Mac Collins differed from Jack Flynt in the emphasis he placed on policy incentives as a spur to his elective office ambitions. He came to Congress to "make a difference" in public policy. And Collins's policy interest derives largely from his prepolitical work. "A lot of my interest in politics," he says, "came from my business experience. When I got to the point where I had the time and the income, I decided to get my feet wet." He entered politics as a successful, self-made owner of a small business, and that prepolitical identity helped shape his representational strategy. "I'm a small businessman," he says. "I'm interested in small business; I work hard for small business." Or, simply, "I'm a business guy." His presentation of self in policy-related terms would lead us to expect, from the beginning, a more vigorous pursuit of policy goals than we saw with Flynt. And that is, in fact, the case. Moreover, because Collins had achieved both his business and his political ambitions through a distinctive combination of risk-taking, self-help, and entrepreneurial skill, it will come as no surprise to find that his specific policy goals emphasize a similarly heavy reliance on individual and private-sector initiatives.

When I met Jack Flynt, he was a fully formed politician in the protectionist stage of his career. When I met Mac Collins, however, he was still a work in progress, a politician in the expansionist stage of his career. Unlike Flynt, he was not a master of memories, reminiscences, and past associations. He was building a reputation. He did not use the word "trust." Nor, relatedly, did he articulate the goal of durable interelection support. To the contrary, he continued to speak in expansionist terms. "In my first race [1992] for Congress, I carried five counties. In my second race [1994], I carried all sixteen counties. I didn't have all of Muscogee that time, but this year [1996], I'm going to carry it, too." He retained this reputation-building outlook throughout my visits.

In 1998, when I asked him, directly, about constituent trust, he said, "I don't think that way. I think people naturally want to question what you do. Your job is to answer their questions." When, that same year, I asked him whether he had "put his stamp" on the district, he answered, "You never feel that way. That's trouble. You can't be complacent. That's why I thought it was time to do some town meetings— that it was time to wade into the people. I haven't done any for a couple of years. So I'm going to spend the first two weeks of January doing town meetings. It will give people a chance to question me. Also, I lost one county, Meriwether, in 1996. That's another reason to get out and visit these places." Policy-oriented town meetings of this sort were never a part of Jack Flynt's repertoire of connections.

Throughout my visits, Collins entertained another distinctively expansionist goal—that of higher office. During my first 1996 visit, newspaper clips told me that he had recently decided not to run for the U.S. Senate.[9] And when I arrived in 1998, the newspaper headline told me that he had just decided not to run for governor.[10] Any higher-office goals he might have could be expected to affect his representational strategy. On the one hand, they would give his strategy a flexibility Flynt never had. On the other hand—because the

road to higher office requires much conversation about public policy—his higher-office goals could be expected to reinforce his strategic attentiveness to public policy.

Contextual Change

Mac Collins's original 1992–94 Third District (see map 4) was the
partisan product of the Democratic state legislature. It had been
carefully drawn to increase the vulnerability of incumbent Newt
Gingrich. But Gingrich had opted to move and to run in a different
district. The district he left behind contained eight whole counties
and parts of eight others. The overlap with Jack Flynt's district was
substantial. At one time or another, Flynt had represented eleven of
the sixteen counties, and he had represented seven of them throughout his career. In 1992, 79 percent of the total vote and 81 percent of
Collins's vote came from Flynt's eleven counties. Sixty-seven percent
of the total vote and 73 percent of Collins's vote came from Flynt's
seven core counties.

The major change in the boundaries of the district since Flynt's
incumbency had been the subtraction of the urban-suburban Douglas County and South Fulton County residents in the north and their
replacement with half the residents of urban-suburban Muscogee
County (Columbus) in the south. In 1992 these Columbus residents
accounted for 15 percent of the total vote and 14 percent of Collins's
vote.

When Collins decided to run, local political judgment held that
the district would be "safe for Democrats" and "safely Democratic."[11]
This judgment was strengthened when a five-term incumbent Democratic congressman opted to run there. "A lot of people didn't give
us a chance," says Collins. "He was a conservative Democrat. He was
strong in Columbus. The state party chairman didn't think we could
win. The RNC didn't think we could win." "Everyone thought I was
crazy." But Collins won with 55 percent of the vote. And he won
again with 66 percent of the vote two years later—against an opponent who outspent him by more than two to one.[12]

Court-ordered redistricting in 1996 took away four of his partial
counties, filled out two others, and added the other half of Columbus. Clayton was his sole remaining partial county (see map 5).
Of his new district, Collins said, "It's been pulled to the south some. I
lost the Atlanta airport. I regret losing it because I have many constit-

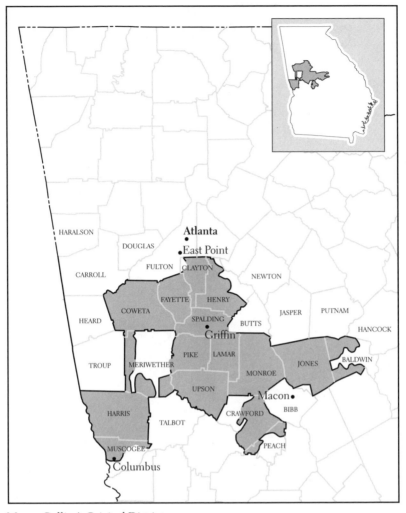

Map 4. Collins's Original District, 1992–1994
(Georgia's Third Congressional District)

uents who depend upon it." But he did not regret the loss of his
partial counties, because the new district was more compact "and
easier to handle." "You could get the votes in those [partial] counties.
That was no problem. But it was difficult to represent. Some people
would go to one congressman, some to another. It was a mess."
Complicating matters more, he had shared each split county with an
African American House member. Collins had no hand in the 1996
redistricting. But, he said, "the Third District came out better than
any of the others."[13]

The "south metro" heartland of Flynt's three districts survived.

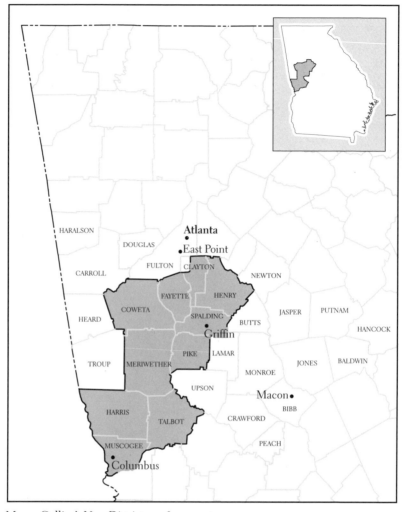

Map 5. Collins's New District, 1996–present
(Georgia's Third Congressional District)

The proportion of the total 1996 district vote from former Flynt territory was 71 percent, and the proportion of Collins's vote from Flynt territory was 74 percent. The Muscogee proportion of the total vote was 23 percent, and its proportion of Collins's vote was 20 percent. So the Flynt-Collins territory overlap remained substantial.

The challenges facing Jack Flynt in his new district from 1974 to 1976 gave us a preview of many constituency characteristics shaping Collins's representational activity in the 1990s—Republican growth, suburban expansion, economic development, and population growth. To these should be added a wholly new factor, technological innovation in two-way communication. These several forces have created a different district and a different set of representational possibilities than existed in the 1970s.

Republican Party Growth and Suburban Expansion

Politically, the growth of Republican Party strength throughout the South was significant. From the 1970s to the 1990s, there had been a steady increase in Republican Party identifiers among white southern voters.[14] Mac Collins was among those who switched, as were his constituents. Ronald Reagan captured the district (with 69 percent of the vote) in 1984, and it has gone Republican in presidential elections ever since. George Bush carried it by 47 percent and Bob Dole by 50 percent, both in three-way races. A strong Democratic district had become a strong Republican district. The regional surge of Republicanism in the New South was nicely reflected, therefore, in the changed partisan balance of the Flynt-Collins district.

Nowhere was the change more prominent than in the district's suburbs. Between 1976 and 1996, the Third District had become steadily more suburban. In the 1970s it was still classified as more nonmetropolitan (52 percent) than suburban (43 percent), according to a *Congressional Quarterly* study.[15] By the 1990s, however, it was classified as solidly suburban.[16] The district's four suburban counties (Clayton, Coweta, Fayette, and Henry) had grown from a population of 84,000, with 35,000 registered voters, in the 1950s to a population of 282,000, with 182,000 registered voters, in the 1990s. As Flynt had seen it, the district's dominant industry was textiles. As Collins now sees it, "The dominant industry is people driving to Atlanta every day." To complete that thought he might have added "or else they drive to work in Columbus," because in his 1996 description of the district, suburbia dominates at both ends. "It's a bedroom for Atlanta on the northern end," he says, "rural in the middle, and a bedroom for Columbus on the southern end."

Politically, the suburbanites of the northern end of the district became his primary constituency. County by county, Republicans challenged, and ended, the primacy of the county seat Democratic elites that made up the cue-giving "governing class" in Jack Flynt's day. Speaking of those one-time Flynt bastions, Collins said, "The northern counties of Fayette, Henry, and Coweta have been getting more Republican in recent years. They are good Republican counties. Even Spalding [Flynt's home county] has been getting more

Republican." He explained his 1992 decision to run: "I saw it as a district becoming more Republican. And I had a [state senate] base [Butts, Henry, and part of Clayton] in the northern part of the district. That's what happened. I carried all five northern counties."

It is hard to throw a political blanket over a working-class suburb like "blue-collar and proud of it" Clayton, which already leans Democratic and "will soon be 50 percent minority," and an affluent suburb like Fayette, which is staunchly Republican and 95 percent white.[17] While the Third District is by all vote measures Republican, Collins refuses even to speculate on relative partisan strengths. "I have no idea; I couldn't possibly guess. My constituents don't wear uniforms." It is probably safest to generalize that the new suburbanites, on the whole, tended to be younger, better educated, more white-collar, less southern-born, more upwardly mobile, more reform-minded, and more independent-minded politically—that is, less attached to parties—than their predecessors in the 1950s, 1960s, and 1970s. It is also the case that these "south suburbs of Atlanta" are described generally as more modest, less affluent, and more rural than their counterparts north of the city.[18]

A 1996 Republican Party study of the behavior of the district's registered voters found 29 percent regular Republicans, 17 percent regular Democrats. and 54 percent swing voters.[19] A 1996 survey of Columbus voters concluded, similarly, that their policy views were "middle of the road" and "centrist," and that "a high percentage (of the group) is keeping its options open."[20] The random sample of "likely voters" in Collins's own 1996 district-wide poll tallied 35 percent Republicans, 30 percent Democrats, and 28 percent independents. By philosophy, however, those same people—53 percent of whom were self-identified conservatives, 25 percent moderates, and 11 percent liberals—were philosophically predisposed toward the Republican candidates. Thus, on the generic congressional ballot in 1996, any Republican candidate held a 53 to 37 percent advantage.[21]

Mac Collins seems totally at home in the suburbs—all of them. He placed his district office right in the middle of Clayton County, the very locale that was so alien to Jack Flynt. And he folds Clayton into the mix. "I carried Clayton [in 1992], but Clinton did, too." "It's mostly Democrats. But I get along with Democrats. They don't throw rocks at me, because I listen to them. I'm the only Republican that wins there." But he adds, "I could not carry it if [Fifth District congressman] John Lewis didn't represent a large number of the county's black voters" (see map 5). In sum, "The district is not hard to represent. I was born and raised in the area. So I just apply common sense to the issues."

His common sense, however, is colored by his business experience. And that, too, seems comfortably suburban. Merle Black and Earl Black have written about the attachment of suburban voters in the South to what they call the "entrepreneurial individualism" espoused by the Republican Party.[22] As a do-it-yourself, up-by-the-bootstraps businessman, Collins is the very personification of that entrepreneurial individualism. And it gives him a strong constituency connection on which to base his representational negotiations in suburbia.

"My strongest supporters," he says, "are small business people and professionals." At a Republican reception for him in suburban Fayette County, I asked the organizer, "What sorts of people are here?" "Mostly small business people, men and women," she said. At a luncheon with fifty to sixty Spalding County Kiwanians, I asked Collins how many would be strong supporters. "All of them," he answered. As we entered the luncheon, one member came up to the congressman. "I'm a Republican," he said. "But I had to register as a Democrat because that was the only way you could get ahead in the community. Now you can call yourself a Republican. My daddy would have a fit if he heard me say that." Doubtless, many another district daddy had suffered such a fit since the 1970's.

Economic Change

When Collins describes the district's economy, diversity is his perception. "Clayton is full of workers at the airport, at Ford, in trucking. . . . There's high tech in Fayette; warehouse and distribution in Henry; manufacturing and textiles in Coweta; textiles, military retirees, and financial in Muscogee. CB&T bank [in Columbus] is one of the biggest in the South." More generally, he describes the economy as "very diversified in types of jobs: airline employees, automobile workers, high tech, textiles, and military." Clearly, the 1970s dominance of textiles and agriculture has given way to a more complex economy. And the sweep of that change was in evidence throughout my visits.

In Flynt's hometown of Griffin, for example, we toured the world-class, high-tech facilities of Nacom, a Japanese-owned company making the electrical systems for Chrysler automobiles. As we entered with the mayor of Griffin, he exclaimed to the congressman, "This doesn't look like Griffin, does it? It sure is a long way from an old cotton mill." In Columbus, we drove by the riverside area once occupied by textile giant Fieldcrest Mills—in the 1970s the area's largest employer, with 3,000 workers. A section of one of its buildings has been preserved as a historic site. But the area has been taken over by the new buildings of Total Systems, a company that processes credit-card accounts for companies nationwide. With 3,500 people and plans for 2,000 more, it is now the area's biggest employer. These changes, from the dominance of textiles to the dominance of high-tech electronics and data processing, were vivid reminders of economic development and diversification in the district.

Driving along outside Fayetteville in 1996, I spotted Jackson Brothers general store—the scene, as described in Chapter 3, of my most memorable campaign event twenty years earlier. "Have you ever been in that store?" I asked Collins. "No," he said. "I never noticed it before." Thanks to his wife, Julie, I returned the next day to have a closer look. And the small-scale changes there seemed to me to exemplify a lot of what had happened district-wide.

Outside, the sign was barely readable, and the windows were covered with bars. Inside, the ambience had changed radically. The cramped and cluttered gathering place had been transformed into a not very well-stocked, not very well-modernized, not very prosperous-looking convenience store. The aisles had been widened, the shelves lowered, and fluorescent lights had been added. Stacks of soft drinks were lined against one wall, and the half-filled shelves contained some canned and packaged staples, ready-to-heat breakfast food, sandwiches, and TV dinners. A microwave and a television had been installed on the other side wall. A refrigerated unit was in the back. The shelves of household supplies were gone. Metal and plastic had replaced wood everywhere except at the counter, where a single antique glass case contained an assortment of penny candy—now five cents each. The case and a single package of snuff were the only bits of memory left.

The store was still owned by one of the brothers but was being leased and run by someone else. It had ceased to be either a community place or, by extension, a politically relevant place. Neither Mac Collins nor anyone else would have his palm buzzed or have $50 to $60 of gas money raised for him there. It was a tiny personal reminder of economic change and the declining impact of rural Georgia.

District Philosophy

A lot may have changed in the district—partisanship, demography, and economics. But district philosophy has not. When Collins describes his district as "middle income and conservative," he describes Jack Flynt's district as well. He describes his strongest supporters, too, as "fiscal conservatives, dollars and cents people, supporters of tax relief." Among the new suburbanites, "liberal" is as damaging a label as it was twenty years ago. Flynt and Collins alike have perceived the district as strongly conservative on sociocultural issues involving race, abortion, gun control, crime, and welfare. And they have seen it as selectively conservative on economic issues such as government spending, trade, taxes, and the environment. The particular legislative or partisan focus within these issue areas could be expected to change. But the overall ideological tilt, whether 1970 or 1996, was one of social and fiscal conservatism.

Accordingly, Mac Collins's overall vote profile is the same as Flynt's. In the judgment of a 1998 résumé, "Collins has one of the most conservative voting records in the House."[23] At election time, Collins is regularly endorsed on the editorial pages of the conservative *Atlanta Journal* and—like Flynt—consistently opposed by the liberal *Atlanta Constitution*.[24] His Americans for Democratic Action ratings for the years 1993–97 were 10, 0, 0, 5, and 5, respectively. By contrast, his Conservative Coalition Support scores for the same years were 91, 86, 95, 98, and 92 percent. Two votes, Collins says, would be fatal at election time—one in favor of abortion and one opposed to a tax cut. "Any vote against tax relief would kill me—that, and partial-birth abortion." A pro–gun control vote would be "bad but wouldn't kill me." Given his personal views, however, the congressman's policy bond with his constituents on these major issues is solid.

In terms of policy voting, therefore, there is not much difference between Flynt's roll-call record and Collins's roll-call record. But in terms of policy development, policy influence, and policy activity, there is a large difference between the two representatives. And that is what makes for the crucial difference in the policy dialogue each conducted with his constituents. More generally, while their voting records were similar, their supportive constituency relationships were very different. One cannot be inferred from the other. And they need to be examined separately.

As the last of his district descriptors, Collins says that "23 percent of my constituents are black." In racial matters, the focus had changed since Flynt's day from the dominantly legal and access issues of desegregation and voting to the dominantly social and economic issues of equal opportunity and affirmative action. The district's black constituents had become increasingly active core partners in the Democratic Party coalition. But the district's white constituents—many of them bringing their racial conservatism with them—had become increasingly Republican. This is typical of the South, where Republican-Democratic partisan divisions on racial matters have become sharper than ever.[25]

Of the district's black constituents, Collins says, "When they hear I'm a Republican, it's like throwing cold water on our conversation." Of the district's white constituents, he says, "Many have the feeling that the government only helps certain people. They often say to me, 'I don't count. The government will not help me.' There is a lot of dissatisfaction with the government. And a lot of it is racial." Although race-related issues had changed, many liberal-conservative differences were still related to race, and race-related politics remained.[26]

Population Growth and Technological Change

Statewide population growth had also changed the constituency context by changing the district's size. From the mid-1950s, when Flynt shaped his career-long representational strategy, to the mid 1990s, when Collins shaped his representational strategy, the population of the geographical constituency had grown from 289,000 to 691,000, an increase of 131 percent. The number of registered voters in the potential reelection constituency had grown from 118,000 to 317,000, an increase of 168 percent. And the actual voting electorate, which included the primary constituency, had grown from 55,000 to 197,000, an increase of 258 percent. Whatever else this population explosion has done, it has altered the possibilities of a representational strategy by creating a new level of constituency demand on the representative. "I have to answer to 700,000 people," Collins often repeated in 1998.

This march of population and demand has been accompanied by the march of technology. A national-level change in communications technology has altered representative-constituency connections everywhere. On the trail, the most striking communication change since the 1970s is the car phone, which allows the representative to respond instantly to individual constituents and the media, and to talk with staff. On the demand side, one striking change is the increased volume of opinion reaching the House member's office.

Jack Flynt faced a level of demand to which he could respond with "the personal touch." He read and personally signed *every* letter that left his office over his signature. His response team consisted of eight staffers—five in Washington, three at home. They did not expect, nor were they equipped to handle, the level of organized policy-oriented mail that is commonplace today when issues reach the active congressional agenda. Once, when a rare grassroots campaign reached Flynt's office, it nearly unhinged him. "I almost got into a fight with the president of the Southern Railroad. I told him that if he ever again sent me those goddamned kinds of letters, I'd call him up, give him some of my stationery, and make him answer them. Those letters paralyzed my office. I could have punched him." Today, in most offices, the names of such letter writers would be entered routinely into a computer, and a standardized letter might follow.

And there would be a lot more of them. In 1997 Collins's Washington office received 14,000 letters, phone calls, postcards, faxes, and e-mails from his constituents on legislative matters—300 a week, sixty per day. And it received nearly as many "contacts" without a return address. One vote brought 190 individually written letters. One grassroots mailing brought 1,000 letters and postcards.

Mac Collins's office staff is twice the size of Flynt's—eight in Washington and four each in the Jonesboro and Columbus district offices. Collins's district director speaks for him at some home events, and another district staffer travels to each county regularly to hold scheduled office hours. Neither form of outreach was practiced by Flynt's staff. When the staff insists, Collins will see constituents—and give them a lot of time—in the district office. Still, the personal touch is not the same. When I heard that the Collins staff person dealing with service academy applications was headed for Colorado Springs for a two-day seminar briefing on how to handle Air Force Academy applications, I could not help recalling Jack Flynt's personal phone calls to his district office from a couple of small stores to expedite a pair of Air Force Academy applications.

Collins's "communication system" has made it possible for the staff to help him connect electronically with large numbers of his constituents. There are 50,000 constituent names and addresses in his computer. A weekly e-mail letter details the congressman's activities for media outlets and interested individuals; whoever reads that letter will perceive a policy-oriented representative. His office has fax machines and e-mail to send messages to constituents and to media outlets. Collins's Web site, which is changed weekly, features press releases, biographical information, updates of his activities, and dozens of pictures with constituents. In 1997 it received 100,000 hits.[27]

However much the incentive and the capacity for ordinary constituent communication has grown, that demand capacity has increased exponentially when utilized by organized financial benefactors among the estimated 11,600 lobbyists running an estimated $12 billion business in Washington.[28] In 1976 Jack Flynt reported $48,000 in political action committee (PAC) contributions from eighty separate organizations.[29] In 1996 Mac Collins reported PAC contributions of $290,000 from 180 separate organizations.[30] In twenty years, the number of groups making demands has more than doubled, and the financial muscle behind their demands has increased sixfold. At one time or another, all of them will want some extra attention, access, and time from Collins and/or his staff. These numbers reflect a total level of demand that can be overwhelming.

In sum, population growth, communications advances, and an explosion in interest group activity have created a changed context for political representation, with consequences we have yet to understand. At the very least, there can be a livelier and quicker exchange of information, opinion, and explanation than before. But a dominating "technological touch" in member-constituency negotiations will not be quite the same as a dominating "personal touch"—certainly not quantitatively and perhaps not qualitatively either. Relatedly, perhaps, assertions of a "disconnect" between politicians and citizens have become more commonplace in the 1990s than they ever were in the 1970s.

What do these several contextual changes add up to? While it may be that in overwhelmingly one-party districts—or in rural districts—a person-intensive representational strategy can still dominate, our provisional guess suggests a different trend. To the degree that changes here reflect national trends, the post-1976 changes we have seen have made it increasingly difficult for a House member to adopt the person-intensive representational strategy of Jack Flynt. They have, instead, made it easier for a member with strongly held policy goals to adopt a policy-intensive representational strategy. In any case, that is the strategy toward which Mac Collins's personal predispositions pointed him. And that is the one he easily adopted.

Policy Concerns

From the beginning of my travels with Mac Collins, the sharp contrast between his preoccupation with public policy and Jack Flynt's preoccupation with personal relationships was unmistakably evident. Collins's public talks were always about his policy concerns. Our "travel talk" often was. Several times during my first visit, he articulated the view that "some politicians' agendas are set *by* the constituents; other politicians' agendas are set *for* the constituents." And he put himself squarely in the second category. In a nonacademic, practical, business-and-political sense, Mac Collins is a policy wonk. He wants to be a policy player. "The part of the job he likes," says a top staffer, "is the governing part, where he can deal with issues like budgets and taxes that he learned in the business world."

Agenda

Collins's policy agenda is shaped by his business experience, by his committee memberships, and by his constituency. Because of the huge impact of Fort Benning on the Columbus area, his freshman committee choice was Armed Services.[31] But the trucking company owner was placed, instead, on the Transportation Committee. When the Republicans became the majority in 1994, he headed straight for the Ways and Means Committee. "That's *my* committee," he says in a tone that evokes the satisfactions of a perfect fit between member and committee. "It was my goal from the moment I got to Congress." "How did you get it?" I asked him. "I lobbied for it. Newt helped. And [committee chairman] Bill Archer liked me." "Why?" "I had gotten to know him in 1992 when he held a meeting with seven or eight of us freshmen to get our thinking on taxes. When he came to me, I listed the tax problems one by one. When I finished, he said, 'You certainly were prepared.' And I said, 'Yes, I *know* about taxes.'"

On the committee, he has specialized in transportation tax matters, especially those affecting the airline industry. His top Washington staffer is an airline specialist, formerly on the staff of the secretary of transportation. Inside the committee, Collins says, "I have had some success" on matters of national and constituency consequence. In 1996 he engineered an extension of the moratorium on the jet fuel tax from two years to four years. He got it through the committee and into the House budget, but lost it to a presidential veto. And after the 1996 election, "Chairman Archer appointed me chairman of a task force on transportation taxes, with a challenge to bring about equity and simplicity. It was the only task force he created. We wanted to change the airline tax. We had five Republicans and three Democrats. I couldn't get any agreement, so I took it upon myself and we drafted a new tax structure, to change gradually. The smaller airlines fought it hard all the way, but it went through. We changed the tax on international flights, too. I didn't particularly favor that, but it was Mr. Archer's part of it. So, in order to get my part, I agreed to his part."[32]

In 1998 Collins used his task force chairmanship to engineer a committee recommendation to change the fuel tax on airlines and railroads—keeping the tax, but taking the revenue from the general fund and placing it in industry-specific trust funds. He commented, "There was no formal recommendation from the task force. The language just appeared in the committee mark. There never has been a formal report from the task force." Similarly, his 1998 ticket tax changes "just appeared" in the committee mark. "The chairman," he says, "takes good care of the committee. He holds the Republicans together." His comments expressed the satisfaction of an emerging policy player.

On the Ways and Means Committee, Collins can be of help to important constituents when their problems fall within its vast tax-related jurisdiction. "Lots of people come to see me now," he smiles. "I used to be on Transportation. I didn't get many people then." Had he not been on Ways and Means, he says, he might very well have decided to run for governor. "I get a lot of good support from being on Ways and Means."[33] Financially speaking, of course, a lot of that "good support" comes from beyond the boundaries of the Third District.

Consider the case of AFLAC, a medical insurance company that specializes in cancer insurance and advertises itself on television as "insuring 40 million people worldwide." Its tall, modern headquarters building dominates the flat Columbus landscape. As of 1996, it faced two legislative problems. First, there was language in the law to the effect that the stand-alone cancer insurance offered by AFLAC would "duplicate" some Medicare payments, thus discouraging potential clients. Second, Japanese insurance companies were not abiding by trade agreements in which they had promised not to sell cancer insurance until 2001—an agreement designed to protect AFLAC's major sales in that country.

From his committee position, Collins has worked to change the legal language affecting the sale of cancer insurance in the United States and to find ways to keep the Japanese from undermining their trade agreement. In 1996 he succeeded in pushing through a provision in a health bill that reworded the law so as to take any onus off stand-alone cancer insurance. And when AFLAC's problem with Japan threatened a very large portion of its international business, Collins went a step further. "I went to Japan last year to see if I couldn't help to make the Japanese abide by the trade agreement. I wasn't making any headway here, so I decided to go to Japan. I guess you'd call that being involved. . . . One of the senators said to me on the way home, 'I sure hope that insurance company of yours takes care of you for life, if you get that insurance problem fixed. The rest of us were keeping count of how many times you brought that up during the trip. You don't give up, do you?' I brought that up everywhere we went."

Later, when "fast track" trade legislation—and his vote—was in doubt, Collins took up the trade agreement problem case in his talks with the president. His efforts on behalf of a major business have not gone unnoticed in the community.[34] AFLAC is his single largest PAC contributor ($13,000 in 1996). And a luncheon meeting I attended—of some Columbus primary constituents—was sponsored by the company.

Dialogue

During my first three-day visit in February 1996, Collins spoke to six different groups of constituents: two sets of senior citizens, UPS employees, management accountants, veterans, and political supporters. In every case, the connections he made were policy connections. He presented himself not as a representative "one of us" or as the carrier of long-standing community values, but as someone who was concerned about current policy problems and who was working on those problems on his constituents' behalf. In six talks, ranging from fifteen to forty-five minutes, he spoke about debts and budgets, jobs, taxes, and entitlements—often in mind-numbing detail. Instantly, the basic Flynt-Collins difference in representational behavior appeared. Mac Collins is not only a policy wonk but also a policy educator.

Collins takes special pride in saying the same thing to everyone. And that is what he did. Six times he challenged his listeners, in the same language, to think about the economy. "The numbers are pretty overwhelming. Our debt is $4.9 trillion. If we paid off the principal—not the interest, the principal—how long do you think it would take to retire that principal? [pause] Thirty years! And who do you think is going to have to pay off that debt—anyone in this room? [pause] No, our children and grandchildren. . . . Now, we can address the fiscal affairs of this country in one of two ways. We can get spending under control, or we can increase taxes. . . . The answer is to control spending. And that's what we are intending to do." To senior citizen groups and veterans, there followed a lengthy discussion of Medicare and the ways that "we are trying to reduce the growth of spending from about 12.5 percent for Medicare annually to 7 percent." To the other groups, there was more emphasis on economic growth.

His mantra was that the governmentally imposed costs of "excessive taxation, burdensome regulation, and expensive litigation" are "reflected in the price of every single good we sell abroad and are killing us in world competition." For small business, "we need to do something to allow us to keep more of what we earn." For the ordinary worker, the problem is "stagnant wages and the feeling of insecurity people have." The message, he said, was simple: "Get the government out of our lives and get production up."

In every case, Collins assumed the intelligence of his listeners and gave them a large dose of information. He described the problems that he felt needed to be solved. He indicated the general direction he would take to solve them, giving the sense that he was up on things and trying hard. He told one group, "I don't want to preach gloom and doom. I just want to tell you the facts." To others he said, "It's not going to be easy. If it was, someone would have figured it out by now." In the car, riding from one group to another, he commented, "I believe in dialogue. The important thing is that you have a dialogue with your constituents." Clearly, the dialogue of which he spoke was policy dialogue.

This early emphasis on policy dialogue remained strong to the last day of my research. In October 1998 the congressman was a panelist at Fort Benning's open house for military retirees, answering the complaints from an assemblage of several hundred retirees about the loss of certain health benefits. On the central question of whether or not the government was violating a contract, he delivered a detailed, but sobering explanation—that there was no contract and no available money, that we had no surplus, only "a positive cash flow," and that Social Security had first claim on available funds. Half a dozen retirees pressed their case, but the exchanges were respectful. Collins took the role of teacher, and he received a long round of applause at the end.

"I love doing what we just did," he said as we left. "I like listening to people and answering their questions. Listening is the most important thing. You pick up information and you learn how best to say what you want to say, how to answer their questions in a manner that puts you on their level. I hope the lady [panelist] from the Veterans Administration didn't get too upset when I said we needed to focus more on health care and less on bricks and mortar. That was a good stop—a *very* good stop." A staffer summarized, "It was typical Mac—straight talk and no big promises." Be that as it may, the congressman does seem to be at his best in situations of unrehearsed give-and-take with his constituents.

Politics

Much of our February 1996 "travel talk" was stimulated by the ongoing Republican presidential primary. Collins's first choice—for whom he had campaigned in Iowa—was a policy soul mate, Phil Gramm. But Gramm had dropped out. "He had the right message, but it wasn't getting through to the taxi driver." Collins shared many of the policy views of candidate Pat Buchanan, but not his style or his rhetoric. "He and I relate to the same people," he said. "We have the same kind of message, but he does it differently than I do. He's too negative." For the three days I was with him, he slowly accommodated to the idea of endorsing Bob Dole. Overtly, at least, that process centered on public policy.

In the aftermath of the bruising legislative battles over the North American Free Trade Agreement (NAFTA) and the General Agreement on Tariffs and Trade (GATT), Collins was preoccupied with trade issues. The policy consequence that concerned him—as it did Buchanan—was the loss of jobs. The congressman recounted "testing" episodes. There was a meeting with President Clinton, for example.

During the GATT debate, I was called over to the White House to talk with the president. I guess they thought I was undecided, although I had pretty much made up my mind about it. I asked him whether, if we went into GATT, wouldn't it cost us some low-end jobs. And do you know what Clinton said? He said, "Yes, we will lose some low-end jobs, but we shouldn't worry about that because we were going to lose those jobs anyway." I could not believe the president of the United States said that. To me, we need to protect every single American job. We should not accept the loss of one job. What he said was BS. He's out of touch with what's going on in this country.

To make the same point, he rehearsed other confrontational conversations on trade—with the consul general of Japan and with an executive of a textile company that was sending work overseas.

"I'm looking for a [presidential] candidate with a message," Collins said. "Not protectionism, but trade; not isolation, but free trade—not some person who will cave. 'If you want to trade with us, you've got to let us trade with you.' . . . [Now] we sit down at the trade table, and we get our britches taken off. . . . We are exporting jobs, not products." He told Dole supporters, "If Dole gets our message, I'll come on board. But if he doesn't get our message, I'm not going to do it." And he faxed one of his own speeches to Dole, "so they'll know exactly how I feel."

His flirtation with the Dole candidacy conveyed the importance of his policy goals. But it also conveyed the presence of his higher-office goals. He wanted to be a player in the broader political arena, and to be recognized as such by other players. For three days, he played phone tag with Dole. "The reason I haven't endorsed Mr. Dole," he said, "is because I haven't talked with Mr. Dole."

When I returned to Georgia in October, he described the outcome.

When we got back to Washington, I went to see him. I remember I pulled my chair right up under his nose. Here I was, one little member of Congress. But I *am* respected in Georgia, for what that's worth. I told him that what the people in the Third District of Georgia want is a balance in the budget and a balance in trade. I told him that in order to get the first, they wanted lower taxes, less regulation, and less litigation, and that in order to get the second, they want someone who will be firm at the bargaining table, to make trade fair and to worry about losing jobs. . . . "Well," he said, "I'm going to be in Georgia tomorrow." I said, "Well, I won't be." I didn't endorse him.

When I got back to my office, I said to myself, "Of course, I'm going to endorse him. I have no choice." So I called him. He postponed his trip a day, and we rode down together. I showed him what I was going to say, and I said, "If you don't approve of this, I won't say anything." He said he did approve. I spoke about balanced budget and fair trade and endorsed him—with all the media there.

So there was Mac Collins on C-SPAN, outside an Atlanta recycling plant, on a platform filled with Georgia dignitaries and Bob Dole. He said that he had talked with the candidate "face to face," that the candidate had delivered on several conservative policies in the Senate, and that he, Collins, was, therefore, endorsing him.

All in all, he was playing out, in public, a web of policy and party involvements I could not imagine with Jack Flynt—partly because Flynt was not as policy-oriented and partly because he was not as favorably positioned within his own national party.

Working People

A distinctive ingredient of Mac Collins's policy concerns, as he expresses it, is his representational relationship with "working people." His 1992 campaign slogan was "A working man in Congress." When he thinks about broad policy at home and when he votes in Congress, he sees himself as responding to, and being proactive in support of, "the average guy," the "ordinary guy"—"the taxi driver" as he put it earlier, and often.[35] On taxes, he says, "I don't care where you put a tax, working people will pay the bill." On jobs, he says, "Fast track isn't about the companies. . . . They can pick up and go to another country. It's about the individual working person who can't move and who gets hurt."

On the environment, he says, "I'm a jobs nut. I'm a believer in manufacturing. I come down on the side of development." To this he adds, "Thankfully, there are not many environmentalists in the district, [and] I respectfully disagree with them." On welfare, he says, "Working people go to the grocery store, they stick to a budget, then they get in line and see someone with a buggy piled high with purchases they can't afford, paying for them with food stamps. Working people are tired of it. They're angry and tired of paying for welfare."[36]

Part of this stance is policy analysis and part is personal predisposition. "I'm a redneck congressman," he told me in our very first conversation. And he often introduced me to groups by saying, with a smile, "He's from New York, and he's come down here to see what a redneck congressman does." Jack Flynt, as noted earlier, used the term "redneck." But his presentation of self was "People might think I'm a redneck, but I'm not." Mac Collins's presentation of self, on the other hand, is "People may not think I'm a redneck, but I am." It is a way of signaling his identification with, and his empathy for, the less-educated, blue-collar, job-oriented working people he has associated with all his life.

"I understand blue-collar folks," he explains, "and there are a lot of them in this district. There is a guy who writes for one of the papers who calls me 'Bubba Collins.' " And the congressman seems to agree. "I'm more populist than Republican. I'm a 'Bubba' Republican." When he first appeared on the congressional stage, a leading Atlanta journalist described him as "the working stiff's conservative."[37] A county campaign chairman described him to me as a "blue-collar Republican . . . different from most Republicans and a good man." And a top aide says, "Mac is perfect for the Third District. It's a working-class district, and he's a working-class guy." These associations have enabled Collins to negotiate a broader policy-related relationship with his working-class constituents than the average Republican member of Congress.

When Eastern Airlines employees lost a bitter battle against owner Frank Lorenzo—a battle that drove the airline out of business—Collins was critical of his predecessor, Newt Gingrich, for not supporting an arbitration board to help the workers. "He would not go to bat for the employees against Lorenzo when he was taking Eastern down. Thousands lost their jobs. They never forgave Newt." "Would you have supported arbitration?" I asked. "You bet I would," he said. "I'd have been right under management's noses." "So why didn't Gingrich?" I wondered. "[Because of] a lack of understanding of the problems of uneducated blue-collar workers by an educated person who hasn't had any relevant experience," he replied. When he got to Congress, Collins had helped to bar Lorenzo from operating another airline because, he said, "the former employees of Eastern . . . have suffered enough from such greed."[38] So, not only does Collins's representational strategy differ from Flynt's, it differs from that of Flynt's immediate successor, too.

With Atlanta's Hartsfield Airport bordering his district, the health of the airline industry is of continuing concern to Collins. When a ValuJet plane crashed in Florida and the Federal Aviation Administration shut down the airline, Collins became an honest broker, working to keep open the lines of communication and bring the two sides to the negotiating table. "A lot of former Eastern Airlines employees had found a second go-around with ValuJet, and I didn't want them to be out of work. It was the workers I was worried about." When negotiations succeeded, "I took the first plane that flew to Washington. The picture of me sitting there on the plane was worth a million words." For Collins, the ValuJet example illustrates his representational strengths. "I can go down to the garage and sit there and talk to them, and I can go to the board room of the bank and talk to them. And I can make them understand the point of view of the working person. I've been there, and I'm proud of it."

The Ford Assembly Plant in Clayton County is one of the Third District's largest employers. It turns out 1,000 Taurus automobiles a day. Its 2,400 United Automobile Workers (UAW) have the strongest union in the district, and an estimated 25 to 30 percent of them live there. The UAW is at the opposite end of the liberal-conservative philosophical spectrum from Mac Collins. But he shows up at the plant periodically—for a briefing, a tour, and lunch. I went with him in 1998. A plant visit is the sort of thing I never did with Jack Flynt, the sort of thing that did not appear on Flynt's 1972–74 schedule, and something he never talked about doing.

Collins set the tone for our visit when he said to the management-union group, "As I told President Clinton when we met for the first time and looked him in the face, 'We have different philosophies. Let's get that out of the way right now and talk!' I like to talk things out. I believe in dialogue." Throughout the visit, we were in the company of about fifteen people—the plant manager, section leaders, union officials, and an economist from the Ford Motor Company in Dearborn. Collins's committee jurisdiction, of course, includes trade, and Ford had sent its "top economist" to the meeting. On this visit, the economist gave the bulk of the briefing—on U.S./Japanese economic relations, and on the repercussion for automobile sales.

An introductory video extolled the efficiency of the plant, the positive interaction between management and labor, and the emphasis on personal relationships in all the plant's activities. These are the factors that make the plant, in the words of its manager, "one of the top assembly plants in the world. . . . They come from all over the world to see how Atlanta does it." After watching the video, Collins repeated his familiar message. "I like your idea that it's the people who make it work, who make it happen. . . . Real answers to real problems are found right here in the private sector, in the marketplace. You are working on the answers here and finding them. I congratulate you." He interrupted the economist's presentation at several points to agree heartily with the company in its problems with Japan. He drew appreciative laughter with his comment that "I owned a Chevrolet dealership once, and I put a sign out front saying 'Remember who bombarded Pearl Harbor? Honda, Toyota, Mitsubishi, Mazda.'" He had visited Japan, he said, and had concluded that the Japanese would look out for themselves, make agreements that benefited themselves, and could not be trusted to keep agreements. The lesson was that the United States had to drive very hard bargains, enforceable with our economic strength. Neither management nor labor disagreed with that general sentiment.

Collins's relationship with the workers at the plant seemed open and easy. He explained part of it beforehand. "You'll hear the union guys holler tomorrow. They know I voted against NAFTA and GATT. They like me for that. So they will listen to me." Then he added, "I didn't vote against NAFTA for them [the UAW]. I voted against it because I think we have to make ourselves competitive here at home before we enter into trade agreements abroad."

But his connection with the employees had a personal as well as policy dimension. At a constituency meeting just the day before, U.S. Senator Max Cleland, a Democrat, had referred to Collins publicly as "the working man's friend." Out on the plant floor, I observed a personal warmth toward the Republican that was unusual. The economist from Ford and the plant manager both noticed it, too. During the tour, whenever we stopped at a work section, a group of eight or twelve workers would gather for handshakes, smiles, banter, and picture-taking. Walking along, the Ford economist noted the easy relationship. And he added, "I just commented to the plant manager that I had never seen anything like it. And he agreed. He said that he had managed eight different Ford plants and that this was unusual. He told me that the guys really like Mac. And he thinks its because there is nothing synthetic, no bullshit about Mac." At one point, a worker came up to me and said, "I went to high school with Mac. Mac doesn't trust the Japanese, you know."

With these unionized constituents, with whom he has little philosophical agreement, Collins has preserved enough of a meeting ground for dialogue. He has left open the chance that some of them will feel sufficiently connected with him to think of him, with some satisfaction, as a representative who comes, listens, and mingles. They cannot say that "he is one of us" or "he thinks the way we do" or "we trust him." But he is not the enemy.

In the final sentence of their 1996 report, the congressman's pollsters emphasized his policy strengths. "He has the ability to appeal to a wide range of voter concerns because of the breadth of his issue involvement and because of the relative strength of national policy issues in his district."[39] Indeed, the unusual breadth of his policy concerns opens up more negotiating possibilities for Mac Collins—both outside and inside Congress—than is the case for many of his equally conservative Republican colleagues.

CHAPTER FIVE

Mac Collins and Connections

Policy, Personal, Party

Policy Connections: 1998

In February 1998 I traveled with Mac Collins for three-and-a-half days. In terms of representational change, the striking finding was the almost total difference between Collins's connecting activities and *any* activity I had observed with Jack Flynt a quarter-century earlier. Admittedly, the sampling problems here are large. However, for the seventeen-month period for which I have Flynt's schedule of district appearances (see Chapter 3), he had no events that correspond to any of Collins's. It is, of course, still possible that some items on Flynt's schedule conveyed less about an event than I would have discerned had I accompanied him. At the very least, however, I am confident that, taken as a whole, no three-day visit with Flynt—at any point in his career—would have borne the slightest resemblance to the Collins pattern of 1998. The difference, again, is partly a matter of personal goals and partly a matter of constituency context.

Collins's schedule during my visit called for nine engagements. When I asked him, at the end of the visit, to rank them for their political importance, he singled out four. "It's close among them," he said. But he placed them in this order:

1. A meeting with the regional administrator of the Environmental Protection Agency (EPA) on the water supply of a large suburban county.
2. A meeting with the administrators of a large hospital on home health care.

3. A meeting with federal, state, and local officials, plus private groups, on regional transportation.
4. A meeting with ten members of the Georgia Chamber of Commerce on federal issues.

When he had finished listing the four, he summed up, "I like to deal with problems affecting masses of people more than problems of individuals."

Taken together, the four meetings, to which I will add a fifth—a reception at Maximus, a child-support recovery organization—were indicative of his hands-on involvement in major areas of public policy, as those policies affected his constituents. Jack Flynt had rarely displayed such involvement. Not only was Collins involved, but he had brought two of his Washington staffers down to give them some hands-on involvement, too. "I want them to get more involved at the beginning of problems . . . so we will be better able to deal with them when they get to Washington." The staffers accompanied him to several events—another policy-related step Flynt did not take.

Collins devoted the April 24 edition of his weekly column, "This Week in Georgia," primarily to a description of these five meetings. It was e-mailed or faxed to seventeen individuals working on the district's four daily newspapers, to its nineteen weeklies, and to numerous individual supporters. Not only was he more policy-oriented than Flynt, but he communicated his policy involvements to a degree that Flynt did not—and could not.

Collins's specific involvements are partly the result of changes in the substance and scope of the nation's policy agenda, which brought more complex regulatory structures and a proliferation of advocacy organizations, and partly, too, the result of changes in the Flynt-Collins district that turned most of its problems into suburban-urban or metropolitan-area problems. Without a doubt, the sheer magnitude of these agenda and district changes constrain Collins to show *some* policy interest—as they did not constrain Flynt. But Flynt's representational strategy was neither directed at nor attuned to policy involvement in the constituency, and Collins's representational strategy is. Collins has chosen, as his way of representing his constituents, to take a proactive policy interest. He wants to be a policy player on behalf of his constituents. It is his choice that directs and dominates his constituency connections.

Taken separately, the five meetings tell us a lot about the numerous small building blocks of a policy relationship between representative and constituents. Taken together, the meetings tell us a lot, too, about the process of representation as it takes place in the constituency. On the representatives' side, these are meetings from which they learn, during which they present themselves and explain their positions, and out of which they accumulate (or lose) increments of support and trust over time. On the constituents' side, these are small, partial tests of a House member's responsiveness, tests that accumulate incrementally and influence ultimate accountability judgments at the polls.

We cannot fully understand political representation unless we know something about the many incremental interactions between representative and constituents in the home context. Each connecting activity, however undramatic, contributes something to the ongoing process of negotiation, which in turn shapes the overall representational relationship. Collins's 1998 connecting activities also suggest some generic increments of a policy-related negotiation process.

Brokering

The EPA meeting had the most direct and immediate impact on Collins's constituents. Here the congressman represented his constituents as a lawyer would, pleading their case with the federal bureaucracy and brokering an outcome acceptable to both sides.

Suburban Henry County had bought, at a cost of $2 million, an option on a 124-acre parcel of land on which to build a reservoir to add to the water supply of that growing suburban county. Because the area was designated as wetlands, the county needed the permission of the EPA before it could start grading. To date, the EPA had not given permission, and the county's option on the land was about to expire. The EPA wanted more "wetlands enhancement" than was provided for in the county's plans. Particularly, the agency wanted the county to buffer the several streams in the area to mitigate wetland damage.

Five EPA staffers accompanied the regional administrator to the meeting; three staffers accompanied the congressman. The EPA staff contributed back-up information, studies, and comparisons. Some excerpts from the half-hour negotiation between the principals follow:

Collins: I'm here to see if we can't save my constituents $2 million and get some drinking water for Henry County. . . .
Administrator: In the scale of things, this is a pretty big impact—124 acres. Ours is a legitimate concern. . . .
Collins: I know where you're coming from. I've been there. I was a county commissioner. . . . The Henry County folks believe they have done quite a bit already to comply with environmental regulations. . . .
Administrator: We have the same problem in other counties and in Savannah. It would help us if we could get some multicounty planning on these problems in the Atlanta area. . . .
Collins: I'll make you a deal. I bet you can guess what it is [laughter]. . . .
Administrator: I'm not sure we've got to have these exact numbers or we'll go to war. I want to work this out. Here's where we think you're a little short under the law. If there's a middle ground, we can save some money. We want to suggest to them that they buffer their streams. We'll put our concerns with Savannah on another track. . . .
Collins: I'll tell them that you are willing to help, but that you have your valid concerns under the law. I'll tell them you are willing to go meet with them at the site. . . .
Administrator: If we can envision something happening, we can get started before this county contract runs out. . . .
Collins: What's a convenient date for you next week?

They settled on a date.

As he got up to leave, Collins regaled the administrator with his own efforts to secure water for his home county. "Butts County never had a plan until I became commissioner." He described sediment problems in the wells when it rained, and pollution reduction in Jackson Lake. For me, his mention of Jackson Lake was a reminder of the evening meeting on Jackson Lake pollution that I had attended with Jack Flynt twenty-five years earlier—at which he had sat with me in the audience and had stood up to be introduced, but had said nothing.

Leaving the building, Collins expressed his pleasure. "I sense a good atmosphere and a resolution." And he thought that two contributions of his own had helped. First, "I think it helped that I came alone and did not bring in other [Henry County] people." Second,

"You noticed, didn't you, that I mentioned that I had talked with Carol Browner [head of EPA and the regional administrator's boss] at [my] committee." It was a hint of his own broader access as a player.

The next week, EPA and Henry County officials met. "The county had to give a little," said Collins, "and the EPA gave them the permit. It was a good negotiation." It was also an incremental improvement in his reputation and a building block in his representational relationship with constituents.

Listening

Mac Collins is a listener. "Ninety percent of this job is listening," he says. "I don't debate with my constituents. Of course I try to explain what I know about a subject. But you can't win a debate." His meeting with several administrators of Columbus's largest hospital was important as an opportunity to listen, learn, and discuss a policy area of great interest to him—and to the House Ways and Means Committee on which he sits.

Listening involves questions of clarification, expressions of understanding, and suggestions that may imply approval, disapproval, or skepticism in between. And the representative processes all the information that is elicited through certain perceptual screens such as personal experience or personal philosophy. As Collins processed information in this case, he had two screens. First, he viewed the hospital as a business. And that led him to understand and to sympathize out of his past experience and his philosophy. Second, he saw the hospital as a provider of care for individual patients. That view led him to probe and to prod on behalf of his broader constituency—and in response to the dictates of his job.

The meeting was held in the context of growing controversy over home health care—a national problem with local repercussions. The recent face of the problem was evidence of provider overbilling of Medicare for home health services. The southern region had been singled out for bad publicity on this score. And Collins had been put on notice by constituent complaints—one of them from a man who had refused to pay his wife's unexpected $32,000 hospital bill and who had visited with the congressman twice on the matter. Worse still, the man had also taken his complaint to the Blue Cross "fraud unit," and that move had brought unwanted local publicity.

The hospital administrators did not like being "the bad guy," and they wanted to tell their side of these stories to a congressman whose support they wanted and might need. They had prepared a formal, three-part presentation for him. And just as Ford had sent its "top economist" to meet with Collins at the Clayton County plant, the doctors had invited a "top Washington lobbyist" for the American Hospital Association to attend this meeting. Introducing himself to me, the lobbyist said, "It is important that Congress get the best information." Collins surely agreed with that.

The first speaker described the hospital's general problem and recounted, in detail, the case of the irate constituent. "When the fraud unit gets into it . . . the mildest mention of us ruins our reputation in this area forever. . . . Long-term care is a complicated damn business—guilty until proven innocent. . . . In the case at hand, the patient may think there is improper billing, but there is not. We did what we were supposed to do, we got the patient healthy, but everyone is coming at the system."

Collins responded by taking the perspective of his constituent and asking the administrators to improve "the system." "What are you doing at the front end to explain to the patient what you are going to do? When the patient gets their bill straight from the mailman, that's the worst. It's the system that puts that complicated bill in the hands of the constituent. . . . People can see those numbers, but they don't know what they mean. The big problem is Medicare's billing. I'd like you to take care of that at the front end, so we don't get it [constituent complaints] at the back end." As a policy middleman between two sets of constituents—hospital and patient—he was acting to increase the flow of information and perspectives among the people he represents.

The second official used charts to describe the hospital's finances, with emphasis on government overregulation in the face of burgeoning overhead costs. "Government regulations require sixteen separate cost reports each year," he said as he hefted an eighteen-inch pile for 1997. "We are an integrated delivery system. I'd like to be able to file one report." Collins commented, "The problem is, we don't make laws for Mac Collins's district." But when the official mentioned "cash flow problems" as they affected "the financial viability" of the hospital, the congressman interjected at greater length. "I know what you're talking about. I ran into the same [cash flow] problems in my little business. . . . My two sons are taking over my trucking business now. I tell them that you can haul every day as long as you stay in business, but that the one thing that keeps you in business is to go after your money. If this hospital doesn't maintain its ability to get its money and meet the requirements of your obligations, you won't survive." Afterward, a staffer asked him, "How could you possibly follow that complicated financial presentation?" Collins replied, "I spent thirty years running a small business. It doesn't hurt."

A third official outlined the internal procedures designed by the hospital to insure compliance with the regulations. She emphasized the hospital's commitment to ethical behavior. The thrust of the presentation was that compliance is complicated and very costly, but that the hospital does the job well and is proud of its performance. Once more, Collins interjected a sympathetic note based on experience. "My mother got out of the nursing home business for two reasons. She got too old, and she could no longer comply with all the regulations. She didn't have a real nursing home; she had what they called an 'old folks home.'" "Our nursing home," said the compliance officer, "has a 'No Deficiencies' rating from the regulators. They should give us the benefit of the doubt and go after the others."

At this suggestion of possible action, the lobbyist intervened. "The regulators know they are squeezing the guy who does it the right way and not squeezing the guy who does things the wrong way." Collins replied, "You tell me who's doing the squeezing, and we'll go after them. I'm not kidding." The compliance official pointed out, "There is a big difference between fraudulent billing and billing error. A billing error is not fraud." The lobbyist added, "The False Claims Act comes into play there, and no business can withstand being branded a fraudster under that act." Collins agreed and said he and a colleague had already introduced "anti-extortion legislation" to provide "safe harbors" for hospitals in the face of Justice Department action under the False Claims Act.

"It's interesting how different people increase their cash flow," said Collins. "The Justice Department has found one—a big stick with a badge. They should not be able to label you 'fraud' without evidence. . . . I'm very interested in the hospitals in my district. And I don't like the way the Justice Department does business. I'm going to go personally to talk to Ms. Reno." That discussion ended when Collins invoked their shared, bottom-line opposition to national health insurance. "Eventually, the hospitals will throw up their hands and say, 'Send me a check, I'll work for you.' I hope it doesn't come to that. I certainly don't want that."

But as his final note, Collins returned to his original prod—that the hospital had work to do on behalf of its patients. "Everyone has to come forward with a billing system so that the patient doesn't see all these confusing numbers. Don't wait for Washington to do it. You've got to do it. The bureaucrats will not. . . . If you can't change the system, then you must find a way to provide an explanation [of the bill] to the individual. . . . I have talked with Mr. X [the complainant] twice already, and I'm going to talk with him again. That's my job."

On the way out, the lobbyist ran several issues past Collins for a quick reaction. Not getting all the satisfaction he wanted, he said, "Maybe we'll talk some more." Collins answered, "I like you. You don't give up." Given the ongoing debate over health care, it was important that the congressman understand the hospital's problems and perspective. By experience and philosophy, he was on its side. But as the representative of a wider constituency, and as a prospective policy player, he would not let the hospital take him for granted.

Back in Washington, Collins did what he said he would do. He wrote a memo to Attorney General Janet Reno about the problems of this and one other hospital under the False Claims Act. He put it in her hands himself, asking her "to read it personally" and get back to him. After some delay, she did. As he tells it, she noted that "when members of Congress intervene directly at the top of the department—especially nonlawyers—it sometimes disturbs the normal process." To this he replied, "I'm one of those nonlawyers, Ms. Reno, and I think there's a major problem with the administration of the False Claims Act." A little later, Reno called back to say, "Your hospitals have no problem under the False Claims Act." Later, when the attorney general was taken ill, Collins called to wish her well, and, he said, they spoke warmly. Musing about success in his job, he said later, "It's a lot of things . . . some of it is what my staff does, and some of it [big smile] is 'Ms. Reno.'"

Promoting

At the Atlanta Motor Speedway, the congressman presided over an "informational briefing" by the South Metro Commuter Rail Task Force on a commuter rail–based transportation plan for the region south of Atlanta. Collins had come, with his key staffers, to promote the project—by publicly pledging his support and by promising every effort by him and his staff to secure funding.

The plan called for the development of an intercity passenger rail system to relieve the traffic congestion that was choking the suburbs-to-city arteries. Under the auspices of the Georgia Department of Transportation and its Georgia Rail Passenger Authority, a coalition of interested and affected people—public and private, state, local, and federal—known as the Metro South Rail Coalition had, with expert help, designed and endorsed a plan. The purpose of this meeting, sponsored by the Clayton County Chamber of Commerce, was to explain the plan to various officials in affected areas. Seventy-five people were in attendance. Democratic senator Max Cleland had also come to the meeting to register his support.

The element of special interest to Mac Collins was the proposed commuter line running south from Atlanta to Griffin, through the heart of his district, and continuing on to Macon. The jurisdiction of the Federal Transportation Administration (FTA) extends only to rail lines where the density of usage qualifies them to be designated as commuter rail projects. The Griffin line qualified, but not the Macon line, so the briefers spoke routinely of "the Atlanta-to-Griffin corridor."

For me, the very idea was another small measure of district change. In 1974 a young Flynt staffer from Griffin had told me that up until the road-building of the early 1970s, "we would never have thought of driving up to Atlanta for a date." Now I was being told that Griffin would be brought within easy daily commuting distance to the city. As the federal transportation administrator said during the meeting, "Griffin is part of the Atlanta system." For Jack Flynt, a child of Griffin, it had been nothing of the kind.

One month later, Collins got "key language" inserted into the House version of the authorizing transportation legislation officially designating the Atlanta to Griffin rail line as a commuter rail (not a passenger rail) and, as such, making it eligible for FTA funds. In the same bill, he secured $39 million of funding authority to help build it.

Reporting-Explaining

Our breakfast meeting, in a downtown Atlanta private club, with representatives of major regional economic interests was another measure of the Flynt-Collins district's absorption into the metropolitan area. The representative of a suburban district had come to report on and to explain congressional activity to the Federal Affairs Committee of the Georgia Chamber of Commerce. Reporting to the local business and civic groups was the major home activity of Jack Flynt, and Collins does that, too. But Flynt would not have thought of reporting back or explaining to the state Chamber of Commerce in Atlanta. Nor would they have thought of asking him.

Collins surveyed the Washington scene for the chamber members, and they asked questions about a lot of policy areas—the budget surplus, Iraq, Bosnia, ethanol, Superfund, taxes. But their common interest, and the issue that drew the most discussion, was the degradation of air quality currently plaguing Atlanta. The metropolitan area was in violation of clean air standards and was facing federal sanctions if it failed to act. Seated around the table were individuals representing public utilities, waste management, real estate, airlines, natural gas, and the chamber itself, plus two political consultants. Each one made clear how adversely the federal regulations affected his or her business, how difficult it would be to meet new Clean Air Act standards.

After listening to their sentiments, Collins conveyed the prevailing sentiment in Washington. "The environmental laws are real," he told them. "They are not going to go away. You are going to have to comply. That's the way it is. You might get a postponement. But that only means it will be 'real' three years from now. There is no way to get around it. You must comply. The answers will have to come from here, from the private sector. People here will have to get together, agree on a plan, and present it to the EPA." His message was very much like the one he had delivered to the Columbus hospital administrators a day earlier. Again he was saying, "You have a problem. Take the initiative and solve it yourselves. The best answers come from the private sector. Don't sit back and let Washington do it for you by default." It was the message of someone with a strong preference for private sector solutions in matters of public policy.

Afterward, in the car, Collins rehearsed the self-evident nature of what he had said. "There are pollutants in the air. The law says we've got to get rid of the pollutants—and rightly so, in my opinion. So what do you do? You get rid of the pollutants! Get a plan; the plan works out; things will change." He expressed disappointment at the group's reaction. "I heard nothing new. They'll be back here next year and the year after and the year after. They're always trying to stop something. They want to criticize everyone else's program, when what they need is a program of their own." With the business group as with the hospital administrators, he conveyed philosophical agreement. But at the same time, he tried to convey the idea that as their representative, he reserved a realm of independent judgment on the policy specifics.

Legislating

In Columbus we dropped in on a reception at Maximus, a private organization calling itself "the largest health and human services management firm in the US."[1] The Columbus office is one of three in Georgia devoted to the enforcement of child-support agreements. We toured the work cubicles of its seventeen case managers, who work with the courts of the regional judicial circuit to provide "a full range of child-support services" to needy parents. The congressman chatted with a dozen or so administrators and interested citizens who told him how grateful they were for his help. "We helped them with a provision in the welfare bill," he said afterward. That is all he said, and he did not designate the visit as one of the important ones. That judgment, I assumed, meant that the meeting involved a piece of completed business rather than a matter in progress or an upcoming agenda item.

Collins is not one to solicit or bask in public kudos for past accomplishments. On my next visit, however, in response to a question about his legislative work load, he volunteered that "we worked hard on the child-support recovery provision in the welfare bill, requiring that the noncustodial parent be responsible for the child-support payment to the custodial parent." And he talked about his own legislative involvement.

On a visit to Fort Benning, I learned that the army garnishees the wages of soldiers who owe child custody support. I liked the idea, and I thought maybe businesses should do the same thing. But when I thought about how Republican businessmen would resist it, I said, "Nothing doing." I went home that night and said to Julie, who does all the bookkeeping for our company, "Did you know that the military takes child support out of soldier's pay?" She said, "Of course, that's what we do in Georgia already. For every person we hire, I have to send the name to the state so they can check to see if that person is delinquent in child-support payments." She had been doing that all along and had never told me. I knew there was one day each month she had called "Mother's Day!" Now I know it was the day she subtracted child support from some of our workers.

When I thought about it, it made sense. It was something that came very naturally to her—one woman helping another woman. I took the idea into the committee and they bought it. Two or three others joined me in working out some language. Since then, several people have told me how much they appreciate that provision of the welfare bill. It was the most heartwarming thing I've done.[2]

Legislative involvement and legislative accomplishment are key elements in the overall process of representation, and each activity acts as a spot weld in solidifying the representational relationship.

These five different policy-centered negotiations—brokering, listening, promoting, reporting, and legislating—are the essential, everyday ingredients of the representational process as it is played out in the constituency. The representative is connecting personally with constituents because he or she has acted, or will be acting, on behalf of those constituents. In Collins's case, we have seen what his actions ultimately were in all but one of these negotiations.

Media

With the possible exception of the Commuter Rail Task Force meeting, none of the congressman's four face-to-face meetings described here commanded media attention. In his next week's newsletter to media outlets, he did mention three of the visits, but all in a matter-of-fact, business-as-usual fashion. For all of his policy activity, Mac Collins is remarkably willing to let his home connections speak for themselves. For me, the Flynt-Gingrich debate in 1976 symbolized the oncoming era of media politics. And, indeed, Gingrich lived by the media. Collins has not followed that trend, however. His media relationships are not very much different from Jack Flynt's—but they are 180 degrees different from Newt Gingrich's.[3]

"Don't talk too much," he advises staffers. "You'll learn a lot more if you listen." And he follows his own advice in his media relations.

I'm not controversial enough for TV. I stay away from it on purpose, because I don't want to do that stuff. The "Geraldo" people called me to talk about impeachment. I said, "No, let [Georgia congressman] Bob Barr do that. He likes it." When I come out of the [party] conference, media people ask, "What went on in there?" I say, "We had a meeting." They ask, "Was Newt upset?" I say, "He didn't look upset." I tell them, "Go ask someone else. You know you won't get anything out of me."

I don't need it. It's good for exposure, but you tick off as many people as you please. Why risk that trouble when you don't need it? I have no problem with it; if they call me on an issue, I will talk to them about that issue. I just don't talk about behind-the-scenes stuff in Congress. I don't get excited about Atlanta TV. Once in a while, I will go on CNN, at drive time—but only on the issues.

Policy issues and policy connections are crucial to Collins. But he does not seek—or ask or need—the media limelight to help him. On two occasions, I heard him admonish two staffers when they were more anxious than he was to push him in that direction: "We don't toot our horn. We just get results." "We don't want publicity. We just want to get the job done." It is a curious—if not an unstrategic—posture for a politician with progressive ambition.

At the end of my visit, Collins said, "Well, you've certainly seen a lot of different issues—from health care to commuter trains. Is that enough for one trip?" I told him that it was. He assumed that issue diversity was what I had been looking for; in fact, I had not been looking for it at all, or for anything else in particular. But I had, indeed, found a number of different issues—because the open and continual massaging of issues is the key to this representative's home connections and his representational strategy.

Personal Connections

Just as Jack Flynt's person-intensive representational strategy was supplemented by his policy connections, so, too, is Mac Collins's policy-intensive representational strategy supplemented by his personal connections. It could hardly be otherwise. No politician can be successful without a mixture of these two base strategies. It is the proportions that differentiate these two congressmen, and it is the change in proportions from the 1970s to the 1990s that is significant. In Flynt's case, inferences were made about the secondary, policy aspects of his representational strategy. In Collins's case, we have plenty of evidence with which to flesh out the secondary, personal aspects of his strategy.

"Mac Collins, RFD"

Collins states flatly that he could neither win elections nor represent fully without his personal connections. "It's important that I'm not highfalutin or high-toned, that I'm just Mac Collins, RFD. I have a reputation for talking common sense. I talk straight, and I don't talk down to people. It's listening to what people have to say. It's access. It's letting people see that you are one of them." His words are spoken in the tradition of Jack Flynt, but without Flynt's emphasis on community elites. Summing up this philosophy of personal relationships, Collins says, "Populist is the best way to describe it, I guess. [But] it's a complicated thing."

Local journalists describe the congressman as "a genial, plain spoken man, given to joshing his acquaintances, a thick set man with a shambling gait and dark cowboy boots." They emphasize his "down to earth" qualities.[4] People I met spoke of him similarly, as "the salt of the earth," "approachable," "a straight shooter," someone who "takes time to talk to people." Those who recalled the Flynt/Gingrich/Collins sequence in the district found personal similarities between Flynt and Collins, and differences between them and the man in the middle.

At a Republican gathering, a man who had worked with Newt Gingrich against Flynt said of Collins, "In some ways, he's a lot like Jack Flynt, and in other ways, he's a lot like Newt Gingrich. With people, he's like Jack. He's done a great job of winning people over, one by one and two by two. When our son was to be married, Mac and Julie arrived at the house one day to deliver a present. It was all inscribed. I couldn't believe it—a congressman delivering a gift! Newt would never do anything like that. He came home a lot, but he didn't take time with people. He had a lot of trouble with the old Sixth District. He was too urban. Ideologically, however, Mac is like Newt." A person who worked for both Gingrich and Collins echoed, "Mac takes time to talk to people; Newt was always in a hurry."

After a Kiwanis Club meeting in Griffin, a television station operator made these comparisons:

South Georgia has produced some of the best grassroots politicians. Herman Talmadge was one of them. And Mac is another. Look at him over there talking to those two women. He's in his element. He's what we call a grassroots politician. . . . Jack Flynt was what we call a "stumper." He loved to get upon the podium and throw his arms around. But he was a grassroots politician, too. . . . Newt was an educated congressman. I don't mean that the way it sounds. But some people use their education and their training to carve out a place for themselves that is above other people. Newt would shake hands with people, but not if he had something better to do.

Collins, too, compares himself with former Democratic senator Herman Talmadge. He even uses Talmadge's stories. The former senator lives in his district, and Collins occasionally drops by to visit with him. "My style is often compared to that of Herman Talmadge," he says. "Last year, they dedicated a highway to Senator Talmadge. There were two speakers, Governor Zell Miller and Mac Collins—at the request of the senator. I like Newt Gingrich. But as between Herman Talmadge and Newt Gingrich, I'll take Talmadge any day." "Newt," he laughs, "wasn't redneck enough for this district, but I am." It is another comment on the importance Collins attaches to the ability to relate to ordinary working people on a personal basis.

Constituent mention of Newt Gingrich raises the question of his influence on constituency expectations in the post-Flynt years and, hence, on the representational strategy of Mac Collins. Everything we know about Gingrich suggests that he introduced to the district a representational strategy that was unusually policy-intensive and the polar opposite to that of his predecessor. Indeed, Gingrich explained his decision to switch districts in 1992 as a desire to locate in a more appreciative, policy-oriented constituency—one where people "are glad they saw you on c-span . . . and with the President in some meeting," thus minimizing the necessity of spending "every weekend in one or two county seats going to a fish fry, Kiwanis or something."[5]

If, in fact, Gingrich did alter constituency expectations about representation, then he made it that much easier for Mac Collins to make policy connections and to pursue his policy-intensive strategy. And if, in fact, Gingrich eschewed a person-intensive strategy, then the unsolicited comparisons from constituents indicate that the relaxed, plainspoken personal connections of "Mac Collins, RFD," were doubtless welcomed. Gingrich, as Collins himself opined, "was less popular in the Third District than he wanted to be."

Undoubtedly, however, Collins pursued his own representational strategy minimally affected by Gingrich. If he was affected, it was as much by the contrast in their personal connections as by the similarity in their policy connections. His basic policy-oriented strategy was close to that of Gingrich, but he differentiated himself from his predecessor by adding a personal touch closer to that of Jack Flynt. In the end, that combination made Collins an altogether more comfortable, more durable fit in the Third District than Gingrich had been.

Connections: North

Mac Collins comes home often. In 1993, for example, he flew home thirty-one times and worked a total of ninety-two "event" days in the district.[6] "I own a home in Butts County, a home in Henry County, an apartment in Washington, and two seats on Delta Airlines," he says. "I'm lucky if I stay in D.C. four weekends a year." But he comes home not because of any premium he puts on personal contact. "I come home to see family and a few friends," he says. Four children, their spouses, and eight grandchildren all live nearby. Sunday is almost always reserved for "family time," and Saturday is often penciled in similarly.

In the northern suburbs where the congressman lives, he is not heavily scheduled. Often he will have only one or two events scheduled on a weekend. "I float around," he says. When I asked what effect it would have if he came home only once a month, he said, "It would have no effect. I have a good communications system in the office. And I make a lot of phone calls out of the Washington office. I may come home Thursday and spend Friday floating around to the coffee shops and spend a little time in the office. But I see very few people. The thinking is 'I don't see him anyway, so I don't miss him.' If I'm invited to something, I go. But there are 700,000 people in the district, and I can't get around to all of them—not even all of them in any one industry."

In suburban Atlanta, Collins's home territory, the local coffee shop is his equivalent of Flynt's country store. In 1996 we dropped in one morning, unannounced, on a breakfast group at the Holiday Inn coffee shop in Flynt's hometown of Griffin. "This is the second shift," he told me. "The early shift has come and gone to work." For thirty minutes, he listened and laughed while half-a-dozen men smoked, gossiped, teased each other, and baited the congressman. They seemed to be a collection of older people who either worked at local jobs or were recently retired. One man owned a grader and was upset because the job he had been promised that day had fallen through. The only man wearing a tie was a retiree on jury duty.

When Mac told them I was writing a book, one piped up, "And I can tell you the title of his book—'Why Politicians Lie.'" Everyone laughed. Collins allowed as how, unlike Newt, he had no $4 million book deal, but he had bought me breakfast, and, therefore, "I got me a book deal for four dollars and fifty cents." When someone said to me, "We'll give you plenty for your book," Collins said, "Oh, oh, I'm not so sure I want to be in the book." And so it went. At some appropriate point in the banter, Collins said simply, "I voted against NAFTA." Everyone nodded approval. But that was the only political note.

"When I'm around," Collins explained as we left, "I try to drop in. I just listen to them. I let them drive the agenda. I never pick a fight. They just love to pick on you, and they'll test you and test you. But I just sit there. There's a younger group at the other end of town. I drop in on them, too, when I can. They are good people." And he added, "They are my kind of people. But I didn't even know all their names. I'm terrible at remembering names."

I remembered how, after his 1976 Rotary Club luncheon in Bremen, Jack Flynt had named, table by table, supporter by nonsupporter, each person in attendance. At the Holiday Inn coffee shop, not only would Flynt have known every name, he would have introduced me to each man there, called each one by name several times, and reminisced about some earlier personal contact with each of them. He was never more chagrined than when he forgot or misspoke someone's name.[7] More than likely, too, the men would have invoked connections to his career. The country store had a wholly different level of personal intensity and political relevance than the coffee shop.

Two years later, I returned with Collins to the same coffee shop to join another shift. "Let's see what's going on at the world court today!" A different group of five elderly men in windbreakers—all of whom, Collins said, "are pretty well off"—engaged in the same banter. They teased one of their number, a former mayor of Griffin.

"Our mayor here had to retire because of a health condition."

"Yes, I did. They got 'sick' of me."

"The mayor blamed us. He kept telling us, 'You don't understand the program.'"

"Well, I wasn't as bad as ——. He ran for mayor seven times and lost every time."

"Yes, one year, they roasted a rabbit for his victory party, and half of it was left over."

Everyone laughed. Said Collins, "The professor says he's writing a book. But I think he's either working for the CIA or Bill Clinton. Can you imagine anyone taking six years to write a book?" Two men piped up. "When you get the book published, you'll have to put one right in the middle of the table." "Yes, and then you'll have to come down here and read it to us." More laughter ensued.

When Collins mentioned my travels with Flynt, conversation turned to the former congressman. It was the only time I heard any such discussion. Collins himself rarely spoke of Flynt ("I run into him now and then. He's doing a little lawyering over in Griffin"). The men of "the world court," however, did speak about him. Each of the five had something to say.

"Jack Flynt would help you. Why, he'd bring Washington down here if he had to."

"That's why I liked him."

"One time I was having trouble with the way they were shipping propane in here. I talked to every state official, including the governor, and I could not get one bit of help. I went over to Jack's house and told him about the problem. In three days, he got it done. Jack Flynt was a personal friend of mine."

"Jack would do you a favor."

"Yes, he's our guy."

I was reminded of Newt Gingrich's tenure in the district when two of them mentioned—only in passing, and not in judgment— Gingrich's ethics charges against Flynt. I took the clear message of their remembrances to be that Jack Flynt's defining reputation for person-intensive representation remained alive and well. Mac Collins reinforced that view when he remarked as we drove away, "That conversation was pretty positive. If you called Jack Flynt, he would return your call."

Connections: South

In Muscogee County (Columbus), the southern part of the district, the congressman follows a more "packed" schedule. "My staff usually gives me a structured schedule that moves me around. . . . Typically, three or four [stops] in the morning and three or four in the afternoon, and a speech at lunch." Collins works harder in Muscogee County because it is the area he had not represented before coming to Congress, and he still retains an expansionist perspective there. "I know fewer people personally than I do at the other end of the district." His first strategic move had been to hire, as his top

Columbus staffer, the woman who had held that position for the incumbent Democrat whom Collins had defeated in 1992. She knows the local scene—the sentiment, the players, and the issues. "When I come to Columbus," he says, "I just ask Shirley to fill up a couple of days."

Collins was introduced to Muscogee County in two separate steps—to the mostly white northern part in 1992, and to the mostly black southern part in 1996. The process of negotiating a relationship with his new white constituency was a blend of personal contact and policy advocacy. His policy conservatism fit nicely with that of his constituents. He certainly believed, though, that his personal attentiveness was an indispensable addition. When I asked him, in 1998, "Have you adapted to Columbus?," he explained, "Yes, I have. It took a long time. The people of Columbus were accustomed to being represented by Democrats. And there were a lot of Democrats in Columbus. A lot of business people were Democrats. The problem was not what I did in D.C. It was because I came from the other part of the district, and they thought I would be more favorable to that part than to them. For five years, whenever they called with a problem, I've been there. Problems with the city, with Fort Benning, we're always right there. And I spend more time there than in any other area of the district." (Four of my nine days with him were spent in Columbus.)

By the time I accompanied Collins to Columbus in 1998, he could say, "I think we are just about as strong in Muscogee County [as in the north]. I've worked very hard down here." He could not have said that on the basis of policy connections alone.

One bit of evidence is the comfortable person-to-person routines he has developed in the county. Driving up to Krystal's Restaurant in 1998, he said, "Let's see if the 'mayor' of Krystal's is here. There's a good bunch that meets here—another world court." When he didn't spot the "mayor's" truck in the parking lot, we left. But later, he talked about the "big group here in town—120 to 130 or so who call themselves 'The Fish House Gang.' They are the good old boys of Columbus. The head of it is a former superior court judge. You have to be invited; you can't just go. I was invited, and I've gone several times. A lot of the highfalutin, deep pockets of Columbus want to join, but they can't get in. The members are all RFD people, and they have a lot of fun. I took Bob Livingston [House Speaker designate when we talked] with me once. He had a great time, and he wanted to know how I had found such a good group." It is not likely much public policy gets discussed at Fish House Gang gatherings, but it is very likely that these personal connections are supportive of such policy-based activities as are relevant for Muscogee County.

Minorities

Not surprisingly, Mac Collins's negotiations in Columbus have focused on the white business community. But Columbus is 38 percent black, the most significant minority community now in the district. And tiny Talbot County (population 7,000), adjacent to Muscogee County and 44 percent black, was also added in 1996. Collins's policy representation of the black community has been minimal. As he puts it, "I have a [black] constituency, 90 percent of whom would not vote for me under any circumstances. It's not me. It's because I'm a Republican. It's not hard to represent them really, because I represent them the way I represent everyone else. They don't want my type of representation. I will not act like my [Democratic] predecessors just to get their vote. They know that."

Election statistics confirm his judgment. In 1996 his eighteen new, heavily minority South Columbus precincts gave him only 20 percent of their vote. And half of the eighteen minority precincts gave him less than that. His overall Columbus voter support dropped from 68 percent in 1994 to 54 percent in 1996 with the addition of South Columbus. The increased polarization of the parties is particularly telling in these figures.

In the face of such policy disagreement, Collins provides some outreach by way of personal contact and personal service. It is the same accessibility-based representational strategy with black constituents that Jack Flynt claimed for himself. The difference, however, is that Collins goes to greater lengths in implementing the strategy than Flynt ever did. The impetus for this change is contextual. With the arrival of the civil rights revolution, the district has seen an emergence of black organizational and political strength since the 1970s. And whereas Flynt was trying to preserve racial segregation, Collins has no such status quo agenda.

The very first event I attended with Mac Collins, in February 1996, transported me immediately into a radically different context from anything I had experienced with Jack Flynt. It was a breakfast celebration of Black History Month in Columbus, attended by a racially mixed gathering of 900 people. The African American honorees were Columbus's own Congressman Sanford Bishop and the guest speaker, Illinois senator Carol Moseley Braun.

Collins had no part to play. His presence was noted, however, because after the coming election, he, not Bishop, would be representing the black community of Columbus. In introducing Bishop, the organizer said, "We are going to suffer a lot from the redistricting. Congressman Collins has big shoes to fill." Bishop generously praised Collins for his help in getting funds for a water and sewer project. Afterward, Collins shook hands with people of both races who came up to him, but he did not push himself forward.

Speaking later about his expansionist efforts in Columbus, Collins said, "I have developed some strong ties down here. You heard what Sanford Bishop said at the breakfast, how I helped them get $20 million for the combined sewer outflow project. He got $600,000 from the House Appropriations Committee, and I got Phil Gramm to bump it up to $20 million in the Senate. I think it will be a model project for cities with similar problems, nationwide." Jack Flynt helped his constituents with similar projects, but not in a cooperative relationship with an organized and active black constituency. And each year since, Collins has taken responsibility for bringing a leading African American public figure to keynote the breakfast.

When I returned to the campaign that October, our day in Columbus involved two more instances of personal outreach to the minority community—neither one of which Jack Flynt would have engaged in. First, we went to inspect the renovation of a new and larger district office. Because he was about to inherit the black community of South Columbus, Collins had decided to move his district office from a circumferential suburban highway to a location more accessible to black constituents—in the oldest section of the city, on a main road with a bus line that bordered the black neighborhoods. He needed extra room, he said, because he was about to expand the office by adding the first African American to the staff, a man who had done constituency service work for Sanford Bishop. It was a minority-related allocation of resources within the district that differed greatly from any that occurred in the 1970s.

A second event, more personal than contextual in origin, was a morning we spent in the poorest section of Columbus with a young Hispanic councilwoman, Mimi Woodson. She had met Collins in

Washington when, as part of a group visiting his office, she had lingered afterward to express interest in his viewpoints. They had decided to get together at home. She is a model community organizer—energetic, brimming with ideas, with a hand in every local institution.[8] "I want to teach and show people that they can organize and take their neighborhoods back," she explains. Under a mutually agreed upon "no media, no publicity" proviso, Woodson took the congressman on a guided tour of blighted, drug-infested areas of her district, punctuated by stops for the two of them to visit with the owners of the only Hispanic market in the area and with the minister of a black church.

Her long-range goal was to educate Collins. Her short-run goal was to close down a notorious crack house and to recover some lapsed state funding for after-school programs for four elementary schools. Collins agreed to help with the latter. He was unusually enthusiastic about the morning. "That was a good morning. That was two-and-a-half hours well spent—*very* well spent." It was an expansionist adventure of a sort that I could not imagine Jack Flynt undertaking—even as part of his person-to-person representational strategy. Two years later, Collins commented that "Mimi got that crack house closed down and got a park of hers opened. I went down for the celebration. I praised her effusively."

The congressman's relationship with his minority constituents is plainspoken and direct. And when he is invited to meetings with his black constituents, he goes. He debated his 1996 Democratic opponent before a group of black ministers in Columbus. As he described it, "Everything they said, every question, was slanted toward my opponent. Shirley Gillespie [his top aide] and I were the only people there in the Collins section. But I answered all their questions." In 1998 he held a town meeting in a black neighborhood in Columbus—"at their request." "All but three of the questions were about affirmative action," Collins reported. "The other three were about minimum wage. I don't support either of them. And I told them so. I said that affirmative action was driving a wedge between people and that it was unconstitutional. A few weeks later there was a three-part article in the paper saying exactly what I had said—that it was not right. . . . It was as if I had written it myself."

There is personal contact in such meetings, but, on the surface at least, no negotiation of a continuing relationship of any sort. The deeply held policy differences are so great that connecting on the basis of national-level policy preferences is not likely to happen any time soon. And in the absence of any policy connections, personal connections are hard to develop. In 1998 Collins spoke about his ongoing relationship with the Black History Month breakfast. "I'm not real happy about it because I feel the tension—that they would rather not have me there, that I'm there because I'm the congressman. And I know they'll all vote against me. I'll keep doing it, of course. And I've tried some outreach—going to the South Columbus hospital and going to build with Habitat for Humanity. There is a preacher there who has helped. But I'm still a Republican to them. It's hard to break the ice."

One of his Columbus staffers saw similarly slow progress on the personal service front. "More black people come to the new office now than used to come to our old office," she says, "but not a huge amount more. That's too bad. We have had spectacular success in some cases—with the IRS and with veterans. I think more blacks still go to [Democratic senator] Max Cleland's office downtown than come to us nearby. I wish the word would get around, but it hasn't." In a strictly electoral sense, Collins's share of the white vote is so large that he does not need many black votes.[9] Still, he wants to be liked, and he is uncomfortable with partisan labels at home. But he has not yet found an opening wedge that would change things.

In rural Talbot County—44 percent black, staunchly Democratic, and carried by Flynt in his crucial 1954 primary—Collins has worked, with some success, to cultivate connections with both the white and black communities. With a one-two punch of Collins-like and Flynt-like activities, he achieved enough success to carry the county in 1996.

I called some of the community leaders, and they took me around on a tour. We went by the schools to meet the superintendent. The school enrollment is 90 percent black. I had been told that the twelfth graders were reading at a fifth-grade level. So I was ready. When we met the superintendent—a black man—and his assistant, he was waiting with a piece of paper. He said, "Here are the funds we get from the government." I said, "What are we doing with them?" The assistant said, "Getting parents involved." I said, "I understand your high school students are reading at a fifth-grade level. Their parents have been through the system, and it looks like they don't care. Forget parental involvement and teach those kids to read!" The whole crowd was floored. It solidified the whites and puzzled the blacks.

It was a Collins-like, policy-oriented negotiating effort.

But there were also some Flynt-like, person-oriented complementarities to his negotiating activity in Talbot County.

I drift through Talbotton [the county seat]. I talk to the president of the bank. I talk to the sheriff—a Democrat, but a good supporter. I talk to the probate judge. I talk to the postmaster. I went to the post office and stood in line while he served other customers. He was as courteous and efficient as any postal employee I ever saw. When I got to the front of the line, I introduced myself, and I complimented him on his work. It made a bond between us. Later, I told the head of the Postal Service about him, and he sent him a letter of commendation. Those little things go a long way to build a bond that overcomes diversity. I have gone to their library dedication. And I have encouraged their area development efforts, because they have no industry. They have noticed all that.

I learned later, from Collins's staff, that the postmaster was an African American.

The congressman's strategic blend of policy and personal connections—with whites and with blacks—won for him, he believes, a toehold in Talbot County. "Clinton carried the county two to one. [Democratic senatorial candidate] Max Cleland carried it two to one. I won by thirty votes, but our total vote was smaller than in the other races. I think what happened was that people said to a lot of black voters, 'He's going to win anyway. Give him a chance. If you can't vote for him, don't vote.' And a lot of them didn't. I could not believe I carried the county."

The traditional small-town context, with a less active black constituency, may help to account for what Collins sees as a more promising opportunity to connect with his new county's racial minority. He remembers growing up in a small town. "I like small towns," he says. "Nobody pays much attention to them. I do."

Overall, Mac Collins's relationship with his district's minority population is a good deal more expansionist than that of Jack Flynt. But only in isolated pockets of the district will his blend of policy and personal strategies help him to forge connections beyond his political supporters in the white community.

Party Connections

In the District: The Party Label

Mac Collins, born a Democrat and first elected as a Democrat, took for himself the Republican Party label. His story of partisan change is a micro-level instance of the macro-level change that was occurring all over his district and throughout the South.

> A friend of mine came by one day and said, "We're going to have a meeting to organize a [Butts] County Republican Party. Why don't you come along?" I had voted for Ronald Reagan in 1980. I had voted against Jimmy Carter in 1976. I had voted for the only Republican who had ever run for state representative in Butts County. I went to the meeting, and sure enough, they elected me chairman. . . . In my first race for the state senate, I lost Butts County. In my second race, I just barely carried the county. You just could not get those people to vote Republican. In my third race, I finally got a good margin in my home county. . . . Many Democrats who vote Republican at the national level still vote Democratic at the local level. They are friends of their local legislators. They identify with them, and they listen to them.

Although Collins was elected to the state legislature under the Republican Party label, he still had to fight for the party label as a congressional candidate. In the pre-primary maneuvering of 1992, another state legislator, also from the northern suburbs, was the favorite of most party leaders. Incumbent Newt Gingrich, who was moving to another district, got the two prospective candidates together for lunch. As Collins recalled,

> He was not courting me as the candidate for Congress. He wanted the other man, who was a college graduate, a lawyer, well spoken, and very personable. I was just some old truck driver, never been to college, cowboy boots, Stetson hat, the whole nine yards. Newt danced around the subject, trying to appear neutral, but leaning everything toward the other man. I didn't say much. Finally, I said to the other man, "It's all up to you. It's your choice." He sat up and looked pleased at what I had said. And I continued, "We can do it with knives, pistols, or a primary—because I'm going to run for Congress." Sometimes you just have to dominate. I did, and he decided not to run.

That meeting cleared the way. Collins's formal capture of the Republican Party label came in a 55 to 45 percent victory over a candidate from the southern part of the district.

In party background as well as business background, Collins is a self-made man. Though it hardly needs to be said, it should be noted that his campaigns are very different from those of Flynt. He has a modern campaign apparatus that Flynt never had—and the kind of money to keep it going that Flynt never sought. Collins keeps a campaign office open and staffed with a full-time person year round.

He raises money in the same fashion—not an extraordinarily large amount, but steadily. "I don't mind raising money. We have a fundraiser in D.C. every year. And the money just keeps coming in." In 1992 he raised $255,000, but as an incumbent, he has been in the $500,000 range. He explains that "all the PACs that gave money to my opponent in 1992 gave to me in 1994." In 1996, 65 percent of his $527,000 came from PACs and 35 percent from individuals.[10]

Another difference with the Flynt campaigns is in the use of polls. Jack Flynt never took a poll, but for Mac Collins they have sometimes been a valuable campaign tool. In 1992 the National Republican Congressional Committee did a short, quick, mid-campaign poll for Collins and as a result sent $50,000 late in the campaign to fund a television spot that he believes turned the tide in his favor. That year he won by 54 percent. A standard survey funded by the American Medical Association in 1996 was less necessary. Since 1992, Collins has not been below the 60 percent level. After winning by 66 percent in 1994, he captured 61 percent of the vote in 1996 and 100 percent in 1998.

In the sense that Collins is not the handpicked choice of others, he is a prototypical self-starting politician of his time. He is no more the product of a local party organization than Jack Flynt was. But unlike Flynt, he campaigns as the loyal Republican that he is. He could not seriously entertain the idea of higher office if he were not. At campaign time, he uses the word "Republican" far more than Jack Flynt ever used the word "Democrat." As his relationship with Bob Dole indicates, Collins wants to be a player in the party. His 1996 campaign headquarters featured a rich assortment of campaign literature from the Republican National Committee, the Republican Federation of Women, the Christian Coalition, and the Heritage Foundation. In 1998, without an opponent himself, he gave $100,000 to the Republican Party—$60,000 to the state party and $40,000 to the national. His party credentials are solid. There is a mutuality between the independent entrepreneur and the modern political party— auxiliary and "service oriented," in John Aldrich's analysis.[11]

At the same time, Collins is careful to keep his independent identity. In 1992 he commented that "I will vote for George Bush, but the only trumpet I'm blowing is Mac Collins."[12] In 1996 he commented similarly, "I fish my own cork. Republicans tend to pack together. But if you want to stay strong, you can't do that." When he talks about certain fellow partisans, he adopts a slightly distancing tone. "We have some real, true-blue Republicans in this district." Or, "If we have a hard Right, then that woman is hard Right." Or, "If I went around the district praising Newt and saying that Newt and I were buddies, that I had followed him in Congress, it would not help me."

Collins refuses to quantify relative party strength in the district. "My constituents don't wear numbers on their backs," he explains. It is important to his own sense of independence, and to his local reputation as a "working stiff's conservative," that he is not beholden to any group of party kingmakers or to any special element of the party. After six years of combining independence with loyalty, he now owns his Republican Party label—almost as securely as Jack Flynt once held his Democratic label. In 1998 no challenger ever surfaced, and he ran unopposed.

In the House: The Party Organization

A similar picture of Mac Collins's party connections obtains inside Congress. Between the 1970s and the 1990s, the pull of national forces over local forces had increased in congressional elections.[13] And that nationalizing trend had brought southern Republicans into the policy center of their party and into leadership positions in Congress. When I first met Collins, the Republican Party had just captured a majority of southern seats in the House for the first time since Reconstruction, and southerners dominated its leadership positions. The Georgia delegation in the House, which had counted ten Democrats and no Republicans when Jack Flynt entered Congress in 1955 (and had numbered eight Democrats and two Republicans when I first met Flynt in 1970), had by 1995 shifted its balance to three Democrats and eight Republicans. So Collins had plenty of collegial support from Georgia. He was solidly and comfortably positioned in the conservative policy center of the new Republican majority.

While the party no longer organizes politics in the district, it does organize politics in the House. There, too, Collins balances loyalty and independence. In 1994 he was elected vice president of his Republican class and chosen as a party whip. He was a 100 percent supporter of the party's Contract with America, although he never touted it publicly during my two visits in 1996. His party unity scores are consistently in the ninetieth percentile: 1993, 94 percent; 1994, 90 percent; 1995, 97 percent; 1996, 98 percent; and 1997, 96 percent. One study found him to be among the six highest supporters of the leadership in voting on the House floor.[14] In 1998 he had the highest anti-Clinton voting score in the House.[15]

In 1996 Collins expressed a desire for modest institutional advancement. "As a whip," he said, "I am part of the leadership. . . . The whip organization usually meets with the chairman of the committee to look at the bill and pass it along, or stop it—the last part of the funnel before legislation goes to Rules. I like it. I'm thinking of going for regional whip." In 1997 he was appointed a deputy whip, thus moving from one of seventy-one to one of fourteen. Within the congressional party, however, Collins preserves a zone of independence. He was, for example, conspicuously late in supporting Newt Gingrich for a second term as Speaker.[16] And he voted against the leadership's budget agreement of 1998.

Inside the party, Collins resists associations that might weaken his independence. When invited to a meeting of the most conservative organization inside the Republican conference, the Conservative Action Team, he went. "I thought I might like to join. I just sat there and listened. They wanted to lay down a mark. I didn't think they had done much research to back up what they were trying to do. I didn't go back. I don't join a lot of groups." In the same vein, he disclaims any ties to the influential, pro-Republican outside group, the Christian Coalition. "I don't identify with the Christian Coalition. I have no problem with them. They give me a 100 percent rating. People look at that and say, 'You're a loyal follower of the Christian Coalition.' I tell them that my 100 percent rating comes because I follow my own views on the issues and they happen to agree with the Christian Coalition. I do not follow the Christian Coalition." He concluded. "I don't fly banners for any group. The only banner I fly is the one that says 'Tax relief for every working person without regard to age or income or anything else.'"

Inside the party, too, Collins is quite capable of kicking over the traces. Consider his lack of support for the leadership's school voucher amendment for low-income students. As he tells it,

I voted against the amendment because it had an income limitation. Why should low-income people have the opportunity when the same opportunity is denied to the people who pay the bill? That's just dad-gummed wrong! The leadership was putting on a big pitch. I was prepared to vote for it till I learned what it was. In the Republican conference, I asked that question. "Why should some students be discriminated against? If it's a good thing—and I believe it is—why shouldn't everyone have the same opportunity? Why haven't we made it available to all children?" There was silence. The leadership said only that they had decided on that level. During the whip check, I had put beside my name, "Leaning yes?" A little later in the conference, I was asked did I want to say anything else. I got up and said, "I sure do. I want to change 'Leaning yes?' to 'Hell no, I won't vote for it!'" A few other Republicans [twenty-two, mostly moderates] voted no, too. Later I voted for vouchers in the D.C. bill because it wasn't national.

To a friendly Republican constituent who called to protest his vote, he took his cell phone to explain his views and concluded by saying to her, "That's my position, and that's where I stand."[17]

Unlike Jack Flynt, who found himself in a declining minority within his increasingly liberal congressional party, Mac Collins finds himself in the center of an ascendant conservative majority in his congressional party. That position gives him the incentives and the opportunities to do what he wants to as a policy player. And he does. Collins likes making policy, and he values the traditional deal-making of the legislative process.

Collins was upset by his party's inexperience with governing and by the consequent impatience of Republican House members with the incrementalism and compromises of legislative politics. "When you are in the majority," he says, "you have to govern. When we were in the minority, I voted against foreign aid. Now it's the Republicans who have to appropriate foreign aid. Egypt and Israel and some other countries need the money. And we *are* reducing the total. So I'll bend, and I'll support foreign aid. Some Republicans don't understand that yet." He was also bothered by the party's excessive use of the Contract with America. "Once we had it, I told Newt that he had to decide whether he wanted to use the contract to win a Republican majority or as a legislative program—that there was a big difference. We talked about it a lot, but he never could decide."

Reflecting on the disastrous 1995 government shutdown, Collins said, "Our leadership was hoodwinked into thinking this president sincerely wanted a budget deal. Our two leaders had no experience in negotiation. One was a professor of history, the other a professor of economics. They were not negotiators." As for the other new-comers, he said, "It was the freshmen who wanted the shutdown. They learned that when you try to piss on the president, you just get yourself all wet."

In 1998 he described one of the still-disgruntled freshman leaders. "He's a piece of work. I saw him the other day, and I said to him, 'You ought to go down to Hertz and rent a backhoe because you are digging a hole big enough to put the whole Congress in.' He didn't say much. He's like a lot of them. He's never been in the minority. He doesn't know the difference between getting something and getting nothing. When I see him now, I say, 'You got that backhoe yet?' "

"The Republicans did not know how to govern," Collins said in 1998. "But we're doing better now." Given his policy successes, he, too, is doing better. Much more than Jack Flynt ever did—or was able to do—Mac Collins has become both a strong partisan and a proactive policymaker in the House of Representatives. And his public political career is not over.

Conclusion

This study has examined changing patterns of representation in the American system of single-member districts by looking at the activities of two members of Congress who represented the same district at different points in time. It has assumed that representation is a process and has examined that part of the process that occurs in the home constituency by means of personal observation of the individual members in their constituencies. These member-in-the-constituency observations have been presented in narrative, case study form, with the intention of immersing the reader in a body of qualitative evidence sufficient to support some conceptualization, if not some generalization.

One motivation for the study has been the impression that, to date, political science research—using roll call, constituency, and redistricting data—has produced a more complete picture of representational patterns at the level of the institution than at the level of the constituency. The hope is that some flavor-filled storytelling from within the constituency might help to fill out our picture of representational processes at the grassroots level. A further hope is that the examination of representational change in one small place might encourage the study of changing representational processes in other—possibly similar—places. While the expectation is that the picture of change presented here may resonate most strongly among students of southern politics, there is no reason why the generalizations about process and change should not have some applicability elsewhere.

The process of representation was approached by examining each House member's strategy for connecting with his constituents and by describing the fullest range of those connections. It was argued that each representational strategy is shaped by the predispositions and goals of the member, by the constituency context in which the member perceives and pursues these goals, and by the effects of a sequencing factor whereby earlier career developments or prior constituency negotiations may constrain a member's subsequent representational choices.

Two distinct representational strategies were identified and labeled—a person-intensive strategy in the case of the member in the early period and a policy-intensive strategy in the case of the member in the later period. It was noted that the personal dominance/policy dominance distinction had previously been found useful in distinguishing both House member "home styles" and senatorial careers across a wider range of constituency contexts. The distinction is not, therefore, a regional one, so there would seem to be no a priori reason why the same distinction among strategies would not have wider application. The point is not that one strategic emphasis is any "better" in the abstract than the other. They are just different. And they appear under different conditions—which we have only begun to specify.

The first incumbent sought involvement in the kind of politics that was grounded in his knowledge about and interest in individual constituents. His negotiating strategy centered on his personal connections with as many of them as possible—to the end that, for the great majority of his supportive constituents, their perception of him (as he saw it) came from their sense that he was a representative "one of us." At various points when he might have reconsidered that strategy, he was constrained by his prior experiences not to do so.

The second incumbent sought political involvement that centered on matters of public policy, especially where he could represent (as he saw it), the strong conservative preferences he shared with a solid majority of his constituents. His negotiating strategy centered on policy dialogue and policy cooperation. And, even though he has entertained higher-office goals, he, too, has seemed constrained by preexisting practices—shunning ever-wider publicity, for example.

While the two strategies are distinct and distinguishable, the word "dominant" is an essential qualifier. Both representatives utilized both strategies. In each case one was dominant, but the other was supplemental—and necessary. The difference was in the proportions. The person-oriented representative could not have succeeded without his policies on race. The policy-oriented representative could not have succeeded without his personal skills. The implication for representatives in general is that they will always use mixed strategies. The implication for constituents in general is that they will entertain no immutable idea of good representation and can be influenced by a member's own choice to accept a range of possible strategies.

Further, while this study proposes that the two most widespread and most basic micro-level representational strategies have been identified—and, hence, might have much broader applicability—there is no intention to rule out the possibility of others. One can imagine, for example, representational strategies dominated by partisan concerns or by institutional concerns.

In the two stories told here, representation is a phenomenon of people, place, and sequence. A given House member represents a given set of constituents in a particular place at a particular time and subject to particular historical constraints. Substantial change in any one of these ingredients will increase the likelihood of a change in representational strategy. The greater the magnitude of any one change, the greater the likelihood of a changing pattern of representation. Which ingredient is most likely to change in any given representational relationship depends on the particular story.

In our first story, a representative with a well-established, person-intensive strategy faced the challenge of a changing context in a rapidly changing period of time. He proved unwilling and/or unable to adapt his long-standing representational strategy to the changing context. He had made a firm choice early in his political career and had followed it in path-dependent, protectionist fashion to the end of his career in Congress. An unchanging personal choice and a sequence of past successes triumphed over a changed context in explaining what happened near the end of his career. He survived—albeit narrowly and for a short time. But it is quite likely that his failure to change strategy accelerated his retirement from politics.

Changes brought about by redistricting were particularly prominent in creating problems for this member. For political scientists interested in the aggregate political effects of redistricting, therefore, the case of Jack Flynt is also a reminder of the potentially large impact of redistricting on *individual* political careers and on grassroots-level patterns of representation.

Twenty-five years later, a large-scale change in constituency context and in pre-political career made it easy for a new representative—who was so inclined—to adopt a different, policy-intensive representational strategy. And Mac Collins was so inclined. He had policy goals, and he did not struggle to adapt to the quarter century of constituency change. He had been shaped by it, and he was comfortable within the changed context and with all its manifestations—partisan, economic, demographic, and technological. His continuous, incremental policy negotiations within the constituency became the centerpiece of his representational strategy.

Collins's partisan comfort level inside Congress—when contrasted with that of Flynt—reminds analysts of political parties that there is a close relationship between representational choices at home and partisan opportunities in Congress. Jack Flynt had to choose between keeping his party label at home and strengthening his party connections in Congress. Mac Collins did not. He developed policy interests early on and was ambitious to become a policy player in the legislature. For him, the partisan-conservative context of the constituency that sent him to Congress was duplicated inside the institution, thus freeing him to pursue the same ambitions in both places.

In the district we have studied, the representational process is now more policy-oriented than it used to be. The reinforcement among personal choice, constituency context, and sequential negotiating activities in Collins's case suggests that the changes that took place between the 1970s and the 1990s have tended to make the person-intensive strategy of representation less viable as the dominant one for current House members. It is possible to imagine rural southern Democrats in the 1970s adopting policy-intensive connections as a dominant strategy, but it is harder to imagine suburban southern Republicans in the 1990s adopting person-intensive connections as a dominant strategy.

Alan Ehrenhalt has described the 1970s as a "transition period" in the development of political careers, during which time it became harder to govern than before—requiring longer hours, more policy entrepreneurship, and more impersonal connections to an impersonal public.[1] From that perspective, Jack Flynt's altered district may have put him on the cusp of job-related changes that ran directly counter to his person-intensive representational choices and to the preexisting patterns he seemed determined to follow. To the degree Ehrenhalt is right, the twenty-five-year change we have witnessed in one district may well be indicative of large sequencing effects that have now widened the possibilities for strategies emphasizing policy representation and narrowed the possibilities for those emphasizing personal representation.

In the quarter century under investigation here—the early 1970s to the late 1990s—a dominating, national-level political change has been the gradual polarization, along policy lines, of the two party contingents inside the House of Representatives. The trend has been for congressional Democrats to become more unified around liberal policies, while congressional Republicans have become more unified around conservative policies. Legislative compromise is now harder to come by. Consensus-building inside Congress has become a less civil, less manageable, and, to many, a less satisfying process.

Whatever one's judgment of congressional performance may be, the roots of the institutional-level change toward polarized partisanship lie *outside* the institution. They lie out in the country, in the districts where the grassroots representational relationships between each individual member and his or her constituents are pursued, shaped, and maintained. Nowhere in the country have these constituency-level relationships changed as much in the last twenty-five years as they have in the South. And the Flynt-to-Collins example helps us to understand why they have changed.

From this perspective, we see that national politics has changed because, in many separate constituencies, representational relationships have changed. To be sure, the impact is reciprocal. National-level changes—in civil rights, in political leadership activity, and in population movements, for example—have had a lot to do with changing constituency relationships. Certainly they did in our Georgia district. But these large-scale changes are registered—as far as Congress is concerned—first in the constituency and only then inside the House. Change inside the institution comes when fresh, change-oriented representatives bring it with them when they enter.

From the 1970s to the 1990s, more and more southern representatives entered Congress as Republicans, and more and more northeastern representatives entered as Democrats. Put differently, conservative southern Democrats and liberal northeastern Republicans both failed to hang on in their historic constituencies. As these centrists in both parties shrank in number, the two parties became less conflicted internally, but more partisan externally. That is the Flynt-to-Collins story. Conservative southern Democrats like Jack Flynt, who survived policy differences with their congressional party by pursuing a person-intensive representational strategy at home, have been replaced by conservative southern Republicans like Mac Collins, who have strong, policy-intensive ties both to their districts and to their congressional party.

Other constituency-level changes in other districts might not track perfectly with those in the Flynt-Collins district. And such changes might not be captured within a person-intensive, policy-intensive conceptualization. But the Flynt-Collins story strongly suggests the relevance of studying political change at the constituency level in order to understand it at the congressional level. This is only one story, however. Other helpful constituency-level stories of changing representational relationships—in selective constituencies—remain to be written. For students of political representation in the U.S. Congress, that will be a continuing challenge.

Notes

Chapter One

1. Michael Barone, "Who Is This Newt Gingrich," *Washington Post*, August 26, 1984; Peter Ostlund, "A Capital Chameleon: What Will Newt Gingrich Do Next," *Los Angeles Times*, August 25, 1991; Dale Russakoff, "The Search for Newt Gingrich," *Washington Post Weekly*, January 2–8, 1995.
2. Richard Fenno, *Home Style: House Members in Their Districts* (Boston: Little, Brown, 1978).
3. Hannah Pitkin, *The Concept of Representation* (Berkeley: University of California Press, 1967), p. 209.
4. Hannah Pitkin, ed., *Representation* (New York: Atherton Press, 1969), p. 7.
5. Heinz Eulau and Paul Karps, "The Puzzle of Representation: Specifying Components of Responsiveness," *Legislative Studies Quarterly* 2 (August 1977): 233.
6. James Kuklinski and Gary Segura, "Endogeneity, Time and Space in Political Representation," *Legislative Studies Quarterly* 20 (February 1995): 18.
7. For a taste of that discussion, see "A Symposium, 'This Old House': Remodel or Rebuild," *PS: Political Science and Politics*, March 1998, pp. 5–31.
8. A nice recent summary is Kim Quaile Hill and Patricia A. Hurley, "Dyadic Representation Reappraised," *American Journal of Political Science* 43 (January 1999): 107–9. A recent treatment of representation involving constituency influence on another legislative activity, committee work, is Richard L. Hall, *Participation in Congress* (New Haven: Yale University Press, 1996).
9. Richard Fenno, *Senators on the Campaign Trail: The Politics of Representation* (Norman: Oklahoma University Press, 1996), p. 78.
10. Applications of the principal-agent idea that touch the conceptualization of this study are Patrick Sellers, "Strategy and Background in Congressional Campaigns," *American Political Science Review* 92 (March 1998): 159–71; Glenn Parker, "Home Style and Reputation Building in Politics and in Economics" (paper prepared for the annual meeting of the American Political Science Association, Boston, September 1998); and Terry Moe, "The New Economics of Organization," *American Journal of Political Science* 28, no. 4 (November 1984): 739–77. Moe's idea of a "residual," or "slack," is akin to the idea of leeway.
11. Fenno, *Senators on the Campaign Trail*, chap. 2; William Bianco, "Understanding Presentation of Self" (paper prepared for a Conference on Congress, University of Rochester, October 1997).
12. Parker, "Home Style and Reputation Building." A comparative perspective is Bruce Cain, John Ferejohn, and Morris Fiorina, *The Personal Vote* (Cambridge: Harvard University Press, 1997), chap. 6.
13. Fenno, *Senators on the Campaign Trail*, chaps. 7 and 8.

Chapter Two

1. Earl Black and Merle Black, *Politics and Society in the South* (Cambridge: Harvard University Press, 1987).
2. "CQ Census Analysis: Congressional Districts of the United States," *Congressional Quarterly Weekly Report, Part 1,* August 21, 1964.
3. Because of the county-unit vote system still in use for the Democratic primary (each county having unit votes according to population), Flynt's victory was won and recorded in terms of a majority of county-unit votes. It was a system that gave the small rural counties disproportionate voting power, and it was later declared unconstitutional. Flynt won twelve counties worth a majority of thirty-two unit votes; he lost three counties worth ten unit votes—Troup (six unit votes), Meriwether (two unit votes), and Clayton (two unit votes).
4. Richard Fenno, *Senators on the Campaign Trail: The Politics of Representation* (Norman: Oklahoma University Press, 1996), p. 75.
5. John Hancock, "John J. Flynt, Jr.," in *Citizens Look at Congress,* by the Ralph Nader Congress Project (New York: Grossman Publishers, 1972), p. 2; Black and Black, *Politics and Society in the South,* p. 65.
6. Strong evidence that a person-intensive representational strategy should be thought of as a general pattern, not unique to Flynt, is provided by Anthony Champagne's very careful study—using different research methods—of Sam Rayburn's constituency relationships. See, especially, chapters 2 and 3 in Anthony Champagne, *Congressman Sam Rayburn* (New Brunswick: Rutgers University Press, 1984). An aspiring congressman who began with a "sacred belief" in "the concept of retail politics" was Bill Clinton. See David Maraniss, *First in His Class* (New York: Simon and Schuster, 1995), pp. 296–97 and chaps. 16 and 18.
7. Black and Black, *Politics and Society in the South,* pp. 23–43.
8. The idea of elite certification is developed in Fenno, *Senators on the Campaign Trail,* pp. 93–106.
9. In the 1992 redistricting, Upson County was removed from the Sixth District, but Flynt did not move.
10. Black and Black, *Politics and Society in the South,* pp. 15, 20, 192, 195–96, 230.
11. See, for example, the conversation reported in Richard Fenno, *Home Style: House Members in Their Districts* (Boston: Little, Brown, 1978), pp. 63–64.
12. Hancock, "John J. Flynt, Jr.," p. 6.
13. Fenno, *Home Style,* p. 61; Fenno, *Senators on the Campaign Trail,* chaps. 4, 8, 9.
14. Numan V. Bartley and Hugh D. Graham, *Southern Elections: County and Precinct Data, 1950–1972* (Baton Rouge: Louisiana State University Press, 1978).
15. *Congressional Record,* 86th Cong., 2d sess., 1960, 106, pt. 5:5331–34.
16. Black and Black, *Politics and Society in the South,* pp. 82–84, 304.
17. Data for 1958 were compiled from "Report of the Georgia Secretary of State, Based on Population Figures, Georgia Department of Public Health," July 1958. With thanks to Charles Bullock. A similar breakdown for 1970 is not available.
18. For the story of that primary campaign, see Reg Murphy and Hal Gulliver, *The Southern Strategy* (New York: Scribners, 1991).
19. Fenno, *Home Style,* pp. 54–55.
20. Hancock, "John J. Flynt, Jr.," p. 3.
21. William Bianco, *Trust: Representatives and Constituents* (Ann Arbor: University of Michigan Press, 1994).

22. "Southern States Roundup," *Congressional Quarterly, Part 1*, October 7, 1966, p. 2357.

23. *Congressional Record*, daily edition, April 1, 1971, p. H2346.

24. J. Anthony Lukas, *Nightmare* (New York: Viking, 1973), pp. 478–80.

25. His 1976 campaign brochure declared that "more than any other Congressman, Flynt is credited with winding down the Vietnam War."

26. Author's conversation with Adam Clymer.

27. John R. Hibbing, *Congressional Careers: Contours of Life in the U.S. House of Representatives* (Chapel Hill: University of North Carolina Press, 1991).

28. The theoretical importance of the party label for the ambitious politician is set forth cogently in John Aldrich, *Why Parties?* (Chicago: University of Chicago Press, 1955), chap. 2.

29. David Rohde, *Parties and Leaders in the Post-Reform House* (Chicago: University of Chicago Press, 1991); Barbara Sinclair, *Majority Leadership in the U.S. House* (Baltimore: Johns Hopkins University Press, 1983).

30. On conservative southern Democrats in Rayburn's House, see Joseph Cooper and David Brady, "Institutional Context and Leadership Style: The House from Cannon to Rayburn," *American Political Science Review* 75 (February 1981): 411–25.

31. Conservative coalition roll-call votes were those where a majority of southern Democrats plus a majority of Republicans voted in opposition to the majority of northern Democrats. Each individual member's score is the percentage of conservative coalition votes on which he or she voted with the coalition.

32. I first interviewed Flynt in 1959, when researching *The Power of the Purse* (Boston: Little, Brown, 1966).

33. Goldwater won the Sixth District by 54 percent and carried Bibb County by 59 percent. It was, indeed, unfriendly territory for LBJ. For Flynt's claiming the credit, see "Southern States Roundup," p. 2357.

Chapter Three

1. Afterward, the League of Conservation Voters official said to me, "We visited with him [Flynt] in Washington and he seemed very friendly and very competent. We haven't asked anything of him yet. We're hoping he just won't fight too hard for the dam. The state is against it now, and we're hoping Congressman Flynt will let it die." He did—and he blamed Governor Jimmy Carter for its demise. Years later, Flynt opined that it would have saved a lot of flood damage. See Richard Whitt, "The Flood of '94; An Ongoing Crisis," *Atlanta Journal and Constitution*, July 15, 1994.

2. On Republican Fletcher Thompson, see Michael Barone, Grant Ujifusa, and Douglas Matthews, *Almanac of American Politics, 1972* (Boston: Gambit, 1972), pp. 170–71; Reg Murphy and Hal Gulliver, *The Southern Strategy* (New York: Scribners, 1991), p. 56.

3. Flynt's remarks are from an interview with John Hibbing in June 1980. By permission of, and with my thanks to, the interviewer.

4. Tidbits of information about that 1974 campaign, from people interested in Newt Gingrich, can be found in Michael Barone, "Who Is This Newt Gingrich," *Washington Post*, August 26, 1984; Peter Ostlund, "A Capital Chameleon: What Will Newt Gingrich Do Next," *Los Angeles Times*, August 25, 1991; and Dale Russakoff, "The Search for Newt Gingrich," *Washington Post Weekly*,

January 2–8, 1995. Also see Jackie Calmes and Phil Kuntz, "Newt's House," *Wall Street Journal*, November 9, 1994; Katharine Seelye, "Gingrich's Life," *New York Times*, November 24, 1994; Dan Balz, "The Man Who Would be Speaker," *Washington Post Weekly*, October 31–November 6, 1994; Howard Kurtz, "How to Really Work the Process," *Washington Post Weekly*, April 3–9, 1995; "The 1974 Elections," *Congressional Quarterly* 32, no. 8 (February 1974): supplement, p. 405; David Broder, "Some Good Men Surface in a Bad Year," *Boston Globe*, June 3, 1974.

5. Cliff Green and Maurice Fliess, "6th and 7th District Races Similar," *Atlanta Journal and Constitution*, August 2, 1976.

6. The man was Frank Pope, whose later death prompted Flynt's depiction of a prototypically strong personal attachment to a prototypically strong small-town supporter: "I probably visited in his home on more occasions than I have visited in the homes of any person in my home community." *Congressional Record*, daily edition, February 22, 1978, p. H1372.

7. Data complied from "Receipts and Expenditure Reports" from the Flynt campaign, Federal Elections Commission, File ID #004626, 1976.

8. "Report of the Georgia Secretary of State, Based on Population Figures, Georgia Department of Public Health," July 1958.

9. "The Sixth District," *Atlanta Journal and Constitution*, October 29, 1976.

10. In 1974 the *Atlanta Constitution* had supported Gingrich as a "liberal." See Seelye, "Gingrich's Life."

11. Flynt did receive $2,000 from the Democratic Congressional Campaign Committee and $500 from the Thomas P. O'Neill Fund.

12. Congressman Larry MacDonald was the most notoriously conservative Democrat in the Georgia delegation. See Michael Barone, Grant Ujifusa, and Douglas Matthews, *Almanac of American Politics, 1978* (New York: E. P. Dutton, 1977), pp. 199–200.

13. Flynt's interest in black voters reflected no change in his policy views. On June 4, 1975, he voted against the extension of the 1965 Voting Rights Act—one of twenty-five (out of eighty-one) southern Democrats to do so.

14. "The Sixth District," *Atlanta Journal and Constitution*.

15. See Barone, Ujifusa, and Matthews, *Almanac of American Politics, 1978*, p. 212.

16. Charlie Hayslett, "Blacks Gave Flynt Victory," *Atlanta Journal and Constitution*, November 14, 1976.

17. Richard Madden, "Congress Has a New Interest for Georgians," *New York Times*, November 21, 1976.

18. "I shall not be a candidate for reelection to the Ninety-Sixth Congress. It has been and is a high honor and privilege to represent our District in the United States House of Representatives since November 2, 1954 in the Eighty-Third Congress. I shall always cherish that privilege and opportunity given to me by the people of our District, to whom I express my profound gratitude and deep affection."

19. Madden, "Congress Has a New Interest."

20. Alan Ehrenhalt argues that the 1970s were "a time of transition" in this respect. See Alan Ehrenhalt, *The United States of Ambition: Politicians, Power, and the Pursuit of Office* (New York: Times Books, 1991), chap. 12.

21. See Gary Moncrief, "Recruitment and Retention in U.S. Legislatures," *Legislative Studies Quarterly* 24, no. 2 (May 1999): 173–208.

22. On Carl Elliott, see Carl Elliott Sr. and Michael D'Orso, *The Cost of Courage* (New York: Doubleday, 1992); on Frank Smith, see his *Congressman from Mississippi* (New York: Pantheon Books, Random House, 1964).

Chapter Four

1. Jack Bass and Walter deVries, *The Transformation of Southern Politics* (New York: Basic Books, 1976).
2. Earl Black and Merle Black, *Politics and Society in the South* (Cambridge: Harvard University Press, 1987), p. 11.
3. Butts County was represented by Jack Flynt throughout his congressional career, but it has never been in Mac Collins's district. Collins kept his house and business in Butts County but moved to Henry County to run for Congress.
4. The relevance of prepolitical careers is discussed in Richard Fenno, *Senators on the Campaign Trail: The Politics of Representation* (Norman: Oklahoma University Press, 1996), chap. 2.
5. Adele Brinkley, "Mac Collins Brings Family Values to Policy-Making in Washington," *Henry Herald*, October 20, 1996.
6. David Goldberg, "Voters Guide for 1992," *Atlanta Journal and Constitution*, October 29, 1992, South Fulton/Fayette Extra.
7. Julie Miller, "Ray Says He's Likely to Run in Shifted Third," *Atlanta Journal and Constitution*, October 12, 1991; Dick Williams, "Redistricting Leaves GOP and Democrats Guessing," *Atlanta Journal and Constitution*, September 24, 1991; Elliott Brack, "Election Held a Few Surprises," *Atlanta Journal and Constitution*, November 8, 1992.
8. Mike Christenson, "The First Year Congress," *Atlanta Journal and Constitution*, November 28, 1992.
9. "Collins Says He Won't Run for Nunn's Seat," *Columbus Ledger-Enquirer*, January 18, 1996.
10. Brenda Rios, "Mac Collins Decides Against Run for Governor's Seat," *Columbus Ledger-Enquirer*, February 17, 1998.
11. Miller, "Ray Says He's Likely to Run"; Williams, "Redistricting Leaves GOP and Democrats Guessing."
12. His opponent spent $1,284,000 to Collins's $504,000. See Michael Barone and Grant Ujifusa, *Almanac of American Politics, 1998* (Washington, D.C.: National Journal, 1998), p. 413.
13. "Collins Says He Won't Run for Nunn's Seat," *Columbus Ledger-Enquirer*.
14. James M. Glaser, *Race, Campaign, Politics and the Realignment in the South* (New Haven: Yale University Press, 1996), chap. 1.
15. It was 5 percent urban. See Congressional Quarterly, *Congressional Districts in the 1970s*, 2d ed. (Washington, D.C.: Congressional Quarterly, 1974), p. 47.
16. "Congressional Districts Classified on an Urban to Rural Continuum" (unpublished analysis, Congressional Research Service, 1993), p. 31.
17. On Clayton County, see Craig Crawford, "Clinton's Shaky Ground: Gone with the Wind in Georgia County," *Orlando Sentinel*, November 12, 1995. On Fayette County, see Brian O'Shea, "Fayette County's New Congressional District Similar to Old One," *Atlanta Journal and Constitution*, April 1, 1993.
18. Brian O'Shea, "Census Says Third District Like Old Sixth," *Atlanta Journal and Constitution*, April 1, 1993; Christenson, "First Year Congress"; Crawford, "Clinton's Shaky Ground"; Gary Pomcratz, "Even If Bush Didn't Carry Georgia, Voters Sending Four Republicans to Congress," *Atlanta Journal and Constitution*, November 5, 1992; editorial, "Best in Third District: Friday, Collins," *Atlanta Constitution*, June 22, 1992.
19. Survey by Market Quest, "Third Congressional District," September 22, 1996.
20. "Profile of Voters Is No Surprise," *Columbus Ledger-Enquirer*, February 14, 1996.

21. "Georgia 3, Survey Analysis," by *American Viewpoint* for American Medical Association, September 5, 1996.
22. Black and Black, *Politics and Society in the South*, p. 297.
23. Barone and Ujifusa, *Almanac of American Politics, 1998*, p. 412. The same assessment can be found locally in 1994, in Mike Christenson, "Collins Victory Record Defines Watchdog Groups' Meaning of Conservative," *Atlanta Journal and Constitution*, October 20, 1994.
24. For Collins as "loyal soldier in the GOP war against big government," see editorial, "In Congress, Support Backers of the Contract," *Atlanta Journal*, October 23, 1996; for Collins as "hardly advancing the broad interests of most constituents," see editorial, "Candidates for a Mainstream Georgia," *Atlanta Constitution*, October 25, 1996; for Collins who "has gone to bat for Columbus in Washington and done a good job," see editorial, *Columbus Ledger-Enquirer*, October 24, 1996.
25. Edward Carmines and Jeffrey Layman, "Issue Evolution in Post War American Politics: Old Certainties and Fresh Tensions," in *Present Discontents*, ed. Byron Shafer (Chatham, N.J.: Chatham House, 1997), pp. 90–131.
26. This theme is cogently argued in Edward Carmines and James Stimson, *Issue Evolution: Race and the Transformation of American Politics* (Princeton: Princeton University Press, 1988).
27. On the use of the Internet by House members, see E. Scott Adler, Chariti E. Gent, and Cary B. Overmeyer, "The Home Style Home Page: Legislator Use of the World Wide Web for Constituency Contact," *Legislative Studies Quarterly* 23 (November 1998): 585–95.
28. John R. Wright, *Interest Groups and Congress* (Needham, Mass.: Allyn and Bacon, 1996), p. 11.
29. Flynt Campaign Committee filings, Federal Elections Commission, File ID #004626, 1976. Individual contributions are not included in my calculations.
30. Collins Campaign Committee filings, Federal Elections Commission, File ID #C00265942, 1996; Center for Responsible Politics, www.crp.org; rep3mac@hr.house.gov.1996. The number of groups was determined in three steps. First, I cross-checked the Federal Elections Commission (FEC) files with the Center for Responsible Politics (CRP) report and found seventy-one PAC listings in both places. Second, I added the seventy-three groups that were on the CRP list, but not on mine. Those were groups whose contributions were only revealed by checking individual contributions—which CRP did and I did not. Third, I added the forty-six PACs whose contributions were in the FEC records, but not on the CRP list. Those were PACs whose total contributions fell below the $1,000 cut-off used by CRP to make up their list of specific contributors.
31. In 1996 approximately 2,500 civilian employees at Fort Benning, with a yearly payroll of $70 million, lived in Collins's district. In addition, approximately 8,000 retired military personnel, with an estimated yearly pay of $130 million, lived in the district. From Fort Benning, Georgia, "Command Data Summary," January 1996, pp. 19–20, 23.
32. Greg Hitt, "Transportation Lobbyists Target House Panel in Effort to Have Taxes on the Industry Eased," *Wall Street Journal*, November 26, 1996.
33. In 1996 nearly all of Collins's $156,000 in individual contributions came from Georgia. But the $290,000 he received from PACs came mostly from business interests whose reach may have included Georgia, but extended well beyond— as does the jurisdiction of his committee. Data from Center for Responsible Politics, www.crp.org.

34. Nolan Walters, "AFLAC Invests Millions on Lobbying Efforts in Washington," *Columbus Ledger-Enquirer*, n.d. (ca. January–February 1998).
35. See Kenneth Cooper and Kevin Merida, "Republican Dilemma: To Defend the Past or Define the Future," *Washington Post*, February 25, 1993.
36. William Douglas, "Mad as Hell; Welfare Critics Seek Leaner—Meaner?— Way," *Newsday*, March 5, 1997.
37. Dick Williams, "Rep. Ray's Pork Barrel Past Is Collins' Target," *Atlanta Journal and Constitution*, September 2, 1992.
38. Jeanne Cummings, "Proposal Aimed at Stopping Lorenzo," *Atlanta Journal and Constitution*, February 6, 1993; Alan Sloan, "Even If Lorenzo Is a Two Time Loser, Congress Has No Right Outlawing Him," *New York Times*, July 4, 1993.
39. "Georgia 3, Survey Analysis," *American Viewpoint*.

Chapter Five

1. "Maximus: Helping Government Serve the People," brochure, Maximus, Inc., McLean, Virginia 22101.
2. See *Personal Responsibility and Work Opportunity Act*, 104th Cong., 2d sess. (1995), Title 3, Sections 8, 15, 39. On Collins's willingness to be educated on the subject, see Judith Haveman, "Coming to Terms on Child Support," *Washington Post*, March 22, 1995, and Nolan Walters, "Columbus Social Worker Testifies on Capitol Hill," *Columbus Ledger-Enquirer*, May 20, 1998.
3. On Collins, see Tim Daly, "Collins Forecasts Tax-System Overhaul," *Griffin Daily News*, July 19, 1997. On Gingrich, see Howard Kurtz, "How to Really Work the Press," *Washington Post Weekly*, April 3–9, 1995.
4. Mike Christenson, "3rd Congressional District Race," *Atlanta Journal and Constitution*, October 20, 1994.
5. David Goldberg, "Gingrich Likes Chances in Sixth," *Atlanta Journal and Constitution*, October 17, 1991.
6. These figures are compiled from Collins's schedules. An event day is one in which he had at least one meeting with a constituent group, as distinguished from district office appointments or private engagements. Such a distinction is necessary in Collins's case, since he frequently takes a day of private time when at home—twenty-five to thirty such days, by my count, for 1993.
7. See the event described in Richard Fenno, *Home Style: House Members in Their Districts* (Boston: Little, Brown, 1978), p. 64.
8. Delane Chappell, "At the Top: Minority Women Leading the Way," *Columbus Magazine*, January 1996, pp. 30–31.
9. Earl Black, "The Newest Southern Politics," *Journal of Politics* 60 (August 1998): 591–612.
10. Center for Responsible Politics (1996), www.crp.org.
11. John Aldrich, *Why Parties?* (Chicago: University of Chicago Press, 1955), pp. 269–74.
12. Mark Sherman, "Primary Winners Face Hot Potato," *Atlanta Journal and Constitution*, June 27, 1992.
13. David Brady, Robert D'Onofrio, and Morris Fiorina, "The Nationalization of Electoral Forces Revisited" (unpublished paper, 1997). See also Aldrich, *Why Parties?*, chap. 8, and David Rohde, *Parties and Leaders in the Post-Reform House* (Chicago: University of Chicago Press, 1991), chap. 3.
14. In 1995 Collins was one of only six Republicans (and the only Georgian) with the highest score (99 percent) in support of Newt Gingrich's positions. See

Dana Milbank, "No Newt Is Good News: GOP Congressmen Spring to Set Their Distance from Unpopular Speaker," *Wall Street Journal*, June 14, 1996.

15. "Leading Scorers: Presidential Support," *Congressional Quarterly*, January 9, 1999, p. 78.

16. "Gingrich Gathers 12 More Supporters," *Columbus Ledger-Enquirer*, January 4, 1997; Jessica Lee and William Welch, "Confrontation Creeps into GOP Meeting," *USA Today*, January 7, 1997.

17. The roll call was designated by *Congressional Quarterly* as one of the fifty-five key votes of 1997. Member votes will be found in Roll Call No. 13, *Congressional Quarterly*, December 20, 1997, pp. 3144–45.

Conclusion

1. Alan Ehrenhalt, *The United States of Ambition: Politicians, Power, and the Pursuit of Office* (New York: Times Books, 1991), chap. 12.

Index

Congressional districts. *See* Home district; Sixth Congressional District; Third Congressional District

Connally, John, 79

Connection decisions: in home district, 4–5; personal, 20, 27–31; policy, 31–33. *See also* Personal connections; Policy connections; Representative-constituency relationships

Conservative Action Team, 144

Conservative Coalition Support, 101

Conservativism: as Flynt's underlying philosophy, 34, 41, 57, 76; fiscal, 38, 39, 49, 101, 108; and Flynt's congressional votes, 38–39, 40, 49; in House of Representatives, 45, 49, 151; as Collins's philosophy, 101, 112, 144–45; of southern Republicans, 151

Constituency: contexts of, 6–7, 51–55; continuous negotiations with, 7; representative's career stages and, 7; durable interelection support from, 8, 27, 30, 40, 42, 59; trust cultivation, 8, 70–71, 93; voting-decision factors, 9; judgments about good representation, 10, 48; redistricting and, 17; county elites, 21–27, 67; party label and, 43; suburbanite interests, 52–53; black activism, 53, 102, 106; black vote solicitation, 76–77; growth of, 102; demands of, 102–5; policy agendas and, 105–9; changes in historical, 151. *See also* Personal connections; Representation; Representative-constituency relationships

Contexts, 5–7; Flynt's changes in, 15–18, 51–55, 125; Collins's changes in, 94–100, 102–5. *See also* Constituency; Representative-constituency relationships

Contract with America, 144, 145–46

Cooper, Joseph, 45

Country store visits, 21–22, 68–70, 71, 74, 100; coffee shop visits compared with, 133

Coweta County, Ga., 60, 64, 74–75, 99; 1974 Flynt election results, 64; 1976 Flynt election results, 82, 83, 84; suburban classification, 97

Death penalty, 92

Delta Airlines, 53, 58, 70

Democratic Party: in Flynt's one-party district, 17, 43–44; Upson County, 22; in House of Representatives, 45–50, 151; Flynt's loyalty to, 49–50; Clayton County, 54–55; conservative defections from, 62; loss of primacy in South, 62; Fayette County, 68, 73; Old versus New South public profiles, 88; Collins's switch from, 90, 91, 97, 141; Third District as partisan product of, 94; black constituents, 102, 139; strength in Columbus, 135; new strength in North, 151

Demographics: Flynt's constituency, 16–17, 22; suburbanites, 51, 52–53, 54, 98; Collins's constituency, 98, 102, 136, 140

District. *See* Home District; Sixth Congressional District; Third Congressional District

Dole, Bob, 97, 109, 110–11, 142

Douglas County, Ga., 52, 63, 64; 1974 Flynt election results, 64; 1976 Flynt election results, 82, 83, 84; representation problems, 87; removed from Collins's district, 94

Draft-extension legislation, 40–41

Eastern Airlines, 70, 80, 112, 113

East Point, Ga., 57–58, 59

Economic interests, 53, 99–100

Education: desegregation opposition, 32; federal aid opposition, 38; school voucher amendment, 145

Ehrenhalt, Alan, 150

Eisenhower, Dwight D., 39, 46, 49

Elections: Flynt's 1976 challenge, 1, 65–86; constituency support between, 8–9, 27, 30, 54, 59; legitimizing representation, 9; Flynt's proven strength in, 43–44; Collins's vote percentages, 142. *See also* Campaigning; Primaries; Presidential elections

Electoral process, 3, 10, 17

Elites, 21–27, 67

Elliott, Carl, 88

E-mail communications, 104, 118

Georgia Chamber of Commerce, 118, 125–26
Georgia Democratic Executive Committee, 49
Georgia Department of Transportation, 125
Georgia League of Conservative Voters, 53
Georgia politics, 13–14, 15; person-to-person campaigning importance, 20; county seat elites and, 21–27; segregation issue, 32–33; black vote, 33, 76–77; importance of House committee assignments in, 47–48; rural-to-suburban shift, 51; Republican institutionalized strength, 62, 97–99, 143–44; Flynt as congressional delegation dean, 65, 66, 87; Gingrich as outsider, 77–78, 130–31; grassroots politicians, 130–31, 149; Democratic local level–Republican national level vote splitters, 141. *See also* New South; Old South politics; Redistricting; *specific congressional districts*
Georgia Rail Passenger Authority, 125
Georgia State Bar Association, 14
Georgia state senate, 90, 92, 141
Gillespie, Shirley, 138
Gingrich, Newt, 35, 62–63, 64, 87, 134; Flynt's defeats of, 1, 63–64, 81; *Atlanta Constitution* endorsement of, 75; debate with Flynt, 77–80, 127; as Georgia political outsider, 77–78, 130–31; media skills, 79–80, 128; district switch, 94, 131, 141; Collins relationship, 105, 112, 113, 141, 143, 144, 145–46; compared with Flynt and Collins, 130–32, 133
Goals, 5, 6–7; and decision to enter politics, 6, 87; and durable interelection support, 8, 40, 42, 59; Flynt's initial, 14, 31, 87; expansionist versus protectionist, 24, 27, 59, 63, 93–94, 138; Flynt's readjustment of, 48–49, 59, 61; Collins's policy incentive, 91–93, 105–15, 117, 149–50; Collins's versus Flynt's, 117
Goldwater, Barry, 49–50, 68, 79
Good-government reformers, 52–53

Government shutdown (1995), 146
Gramm, Phil, 109, 137
Grassroots politicians, 130–31, 149
Greenbrier shopping mall, 56
Griffin, Ga., 27, 29, 30, 125; as Flynt's hometown, 13, 19; economic changes, 99–100; Collins's coffee shop visit, 132–34
Griffin Judicial Circuit, 14
Gun control legislation, 38, 74, 101
Gunnells, Howell, 22
Gunnells and Sons general store, 21

Haralson County, Ga., 65, 66; 1974 Flynt election results, 64; 1976 Flynt election results, 82
Hawe, Don, 66
Heard County, Ga., 60; 1974 Flynt election results, 64; 1976 Flynt election results, 82, 83
Henry County, Ga., 60, 64, 99; elites, 24–27; 1974 Flynt election results, 64; 1976 Flynt election results, 82, 83, 84; suburban classification, 97; water supply brokering, 119–21; Collins's home in, 132
Heritage Foundation, 142
Higher-office goal, 93–94
High-tech industry, 99, 100
Hill, Guy, 58
Hispanic constituents, 137–38
History of Upson County, 24
Holiday Inn coffee shop, 132–34
Home district: changes during incumbency, 2, 15–18; connection decisions, 4, 31–33; strategy and style, 5; constituency context, 6–7; career in progress and, 7; one-party, 17; redistricting, 17, 51–52; local communication centers, 21, 133; county seat elites, 21–27; party label, 43–45; Flynt/Gingrich/Collins sequence, 130
Home district, Collins's. *See* Third Congressional District
Home district, Flynt's. *See* Sixth Congressional District
Home health care, 121–24
House Committee on Committees, 48

House Committee on Standards
and Official Ethics. *See* Ethics
Committee
House of Representatives, Georgia, 13,
15, 43
House of Representatives, U.S.: Flynt's
election to, 1, 13, 59, 81–86; election
system, 3; Southern Manifesto, 32;
Flynt's voting record, 38–40, 49;
individual institutional careers in,
42, 45, 47–49; party organization in,
42–43, 45–50, 105, 143–46, 150; conservative coalition, 49; Democratic
voting unity score, 49; Flynt's Appropriations Committee seniority, 61,
62, 66; Flynt's increased influence
in, 62, 66; Collins's election to, 90,
92; Collins's committee appointments, 99, 105; Collins's voting
record, 101, 144–45; Collins's staff,
103, 137; Collins's legislative work-
load, 127–28; southern Republican
leadership positions, 143–44; Collins
as Republican whip, 144; party
polarization in, 151. *See also specific
committees*
Humphrey, Hubert, 50

Incumbency: district changes during,
2, 54; campaign emphasis on, 65, 66,
75; as fund-raising aid, 142
Interest groups. *See* Lobbyists
Interstate and Foreign Commerce
Committee, 46, 48
Issues. *See* Policy connections

Jackson, Robert, 69
Jackson, Will, 69, 73
Jackson Brothers general store, 68–70,
74, 80, 81, 100
Jackson Lake, 120
Japanese trade, 107, 110, 114
Jasper County, Ga., 64; 1974 Flynt
election results, 64; 1976 Flynt elec-
tion results, 82, 83, 84
Jobs. *See* Workers' issues
Johnson, Lyndon, 49–50
Jonesboro, Ga., 103
Jones County, Ga., 73

Kelly, Sergeant, 24–25
Kennedy, John, 47, 49
Krystal's Restaurant, 135
Kuklinski, James, 3

Lamar County, Ga., 64; 1974 Flynt
election results, 64; 1976 Flynt elec-
tion results, 82, 83
League of Women Voters, 37
Lewis, John, 98–99
Liberalism: potential challengers to
Flynt, 35; Flynt's low voting score,
38–39; House Democratic faction,
45; House legislation, 47; as damag-
ing label, 101; House Democratic
trend toward, 151
Livingston, Bob, 135–36
Lobbyists, 104, 122, 123, 124
Lorenzo, Frank, 112

McCormack, John, 39, 46
MacDonald, Larry, 76
McDonough, Ga. (Henry County
seat), 24–27, 70
McElwaney, King, 58
Macon, Ga., 17, 18, 19, 27, 51, 61, 125
Macon League of Women Voters, 37
Maximus, 118, 127
Media: Flynt's problems with, 1, 42, 75,
78, 79, 80, 86; television campaign
advertising, 67, 142; Flynt-Gingrich
televised debate, 78–79, 128; Col-
lins's relationship with, 104, 128–29;
reactions to Collins, 130–31
Medicare, 38, 106, 108, 121, 122
Meriwether County, Ga., 73, 93
Metro South Rail Coalition, 125
Miller, Zell, 131
Mills, Wilbur, 19
Monroe County, Ga., 73
Morrow, Ga., 78
Moseley Braun, Carol, 137
Mt. Gilead Baptist Church, 57
Muscogee County, Ga., 93, 94, 96, 99,
134–36

Nacom (company), 99
Name recognition, 10
National Endowments for the Arts and
Humanities, 30

stituency, 89, 94–95, 136, 137; aggregate political effects of, 149
Reid, Marvin, 58
Relationships. *See* Personal connections; Representative-constituency relationships
Reno, Janet, 123, 124
Representation: changes in, xi; definitions of, 3; pattern choices, 5; goals and contexts, 5–7; careers and negotiation, 7–10; interelection support relationship, 8, 40, 42, 54, 59; legitimization by elections, 9; responsiveness tests, 9, 39–40; as process, 10–11, 17, 147–48; context transitions, 15–18; campaign interrelationship, 17–18, 26–27; personal accessibility and, 21; tangible accomplishments and, 23; personal service and, 28; party label and, 43; policy-driven, 117–40, 150. *See also* Constituency; Personal connections; Representative-constituency relationships
Representative-constituency relationships, 8–9; over period of time, 2, 10; trust cultivation in, 8, 10, 28, 35, 39, 58, 74, 93; interelection support and, 8, 27, 40, 54; negotiation in, 8–10; context of Flynt's, 15–18, 37–38; changing district challenge to, 15–18, 55–59, 61, 70–71; accountability and, 17, 119; campaign approaches, 17–21, 25–27, 65–81; elite certification of, 21; local network of contacts for, 22–23; personal services and, 27–31, 45; African Americans and, 29, 136–40; policy agendas and, 32–33, 105–9, 117–29; common interests underlying, 37–38, 65–66; congressional voting leeway and, 39–40, 47; institutional power and, 48; context changes of Flynt's, 53–55, 61–62; Collins's approach to, 93–94, 99, 103–5, 107–9, 111–15, 117–19, 129–40; communications technology and, 102–5; brokering of, 119–21; legislative accomplishments and, 127–28; Gingrich's policy-intensive approach to, 131; current changes in, 151. *See also* Personal connections

Republican Federation of Women, 142
Republican National Committee, 142
Republican Party: Flynt challengers, 17, 43–44, 57, 62–63, 75–81; Flynt policy similarities to, 49; Flynt district reorganization and, 53, 62, 96; new strength in South, 62, 97–99, 143–44, 151; New South policy-driven politicians, 88; Collins's switch to, 90, 97, 141; suburban strength of, 97–98, 99; Third District voters, 98; and racial conservativism, 102; House control by, 105, 145–46; and 1996 presidential primary, 109–11; as Collins label, 142–46; and House conservative trend, 151
Reputation, 10
Responsiveness: definitions of, 3; factors building, 9
Rhodes, John, 79
Rotary Club speech (Bremen, Ga.), 65–66, 80, 81, 133
Rules Committee: enlargement issue, 39, 47–48
Russian wheat shipments, 39–40

Schools. *See* Education
Segregation. *See* Racial segregation
Segura, Gary, 3
Senate, U.S., 93
Sewer outflow project (Columbus, Ga.), 137
Sharpsburg, Battle of, 24–25
Shopping center campaigning, 56–57, 68, 70, 80, 81
Single-member-district electoral system, 3
Sixth Congressional District (Flynt's district): original composition as Fourth District, 15–17; black constituents and voters, 16, 17, 33, 52, 76–77, 85; maps, 16, 18, 52; as redistricted transitional district, 17, 18, 22, 51–64; economic interests, 20; county history research, 21; Upson County elites, 21–24; country store network of contacts, 22; staff, 27, 28, 77, 103; casework, 27–31; speech themes, 34–38; Vietnam War issue,

40–41; Democratic Party label, 43–45; party connections, 43–45, 150; population increase, 51; suburbanization of, 51–55, 96; issue conflict, 53; redistricting challenges, 55–59, 73–74, 149; campaign approach in, 57–58, 66–81; vote percentages by county, 64, 82, 83; civil rights movement's impact on, 77; Gingrich as outsider in, 77–78, 130, 131; overlap with Collins's district, 94, 96
Smith, Frank, 88
Smith, Snake, 71
Social Security, 109
Solicitor general, Georgia, 13, 15, 22, 29
South Columbus, Ga., 137, 139
Southern Manifesto, 32
Southern political transition, 15–18. *See also* New South; Old South politics
South Fulton County, Ga., 52, 55–56, 60; 1974 Flynt election results, 64; Flynt district office, 65; Flynt appearances, 67, 78, 81; black voters, 76–77, 85; 1976 Flynt election results, 82, 83; representation problems, 87; removal from Collins's district, 94
South Metro Commuter Rail Task Force, 124–25
Spalding County, Ga., 16, 30, 44, 60, 64; 1974 Flynt election results, 64; 1976 Flynt election results, 82, 83; Republican strength in, 97–98, 99
Speeches: Flynt themes, 34–38, 65–66; Flynt's Vietnam policy change, 40–41; Flynt's in new district, 57–59; Flynt's 1976 campaign, 65; Collins's policy-centered, 105
Sprewell Bluff Dam, 53, 76
Starrs Mill, Ga., 68, 71–72
Suburbs, 51–58, 60, 61–62, 78, 96; Flynt's weakness in, 63–64, 70–71, 80, 82, 84, 85; expansion of, 97–99, 125–26; north versus south of Atlanta, 98; Collins's policy promotion of, 124–25; Collins's home territory and, 132–33
Supportive constituencies, 7
Supreme Court, U.S.: one man/one

vote ruling, 17; school desegregation ruling, 32

Talbot County, Ga., 136, 139–40
Tallapoosa, Ga., 66
Talmadge, Herman, 72, 78, 130, 131
Taxation, 105, 106, 111; support for cuts, 101
Technology. *See* Communications technology; High-tech industry
Television. *See* Media
Textile industry, 19, 20, 22, 49, 97, 99, 100
Third Congressional District (Collins's district), 89, 92, 94–97; overlap with Flynt's district, 94, 96; changes in, 94–100; maps, 95, 96; suburbanization of, 97–99; Republican Party voters, 98, 99; economic diversity, 99–100; conservative philosophy of, 101–2; black constituents, 102, 136–40; staff, 103; constituent and media communications, 103–5; as working-class district, 112; commuter line promotion, 125; frequent returns to, 132; Gingrich's lack of popularity in, 132; party connections, 141–43, 150
Thomaston, Ga. (Upson County seat), 21, 22, 70
Total Systems (company), 100
Town meetings, 93, 138
Trade issues, 107, 109–10, 114
Transportation Committee, 105
Troup County, Ga., 44, 60, 73
Trust, 8, 10, 28, 35, 58, 93; and House voting leeway, 39–40; building over time, 74

Union City, Ga., 78, 81
Unions, 113
United Auto Workers, 113–14
University of Georgia, 13
Upson County, Ga., 73; elites, 21–24; demographics, 22; Flint River dam project, 53

Valujet plane crash, 113
Vietnam War, 31, 34, 35, 40–42
Villa Rica, Ga., 66
Voting decisions: in House, 4, 38–40,